Route 66
A Guiding Light

10th Anniversary of Kiwis Ride Across America
(2013-2023)

(A Biker's Illustrated Experience)

Nigel M Sainsbury

Copyright © 2024 by Nigel M. Sainsbury

All rights reserved. No part of this book may be reproduced or transmitted in any form or by any means, electronic or mechanical, including photocopying, recording, or by any information storage and retrieval system, without permission in writing from the publisher.

Publisher – Nigel Sainsbury Consulting LLC – Fairfax, VA
ISBN: 978-1-7349665-3-4
eBook ISBN: 978-1-7349665-6-5
Library of Congress Control Number: 2024903042
Title: *Route 66: A Guiding Light*
Nigel M. Sainsbury
Available formats: eBook | Paperback distribution
2024
Printed in the USA

Websites:
www.nigelsainsburyconsulting.com
www.mybikerauthor.com

Dedication

This book is dedicated to all the people who made a squiggly line on a road map, an iconic piece of America. And to Alex, Sid, Surtz, Shag, Paul, and Ian, who made my #1 bucket list item such an enjoyable and memorable experience.

Acknowledgements

To all the wonderful people we met, the food we ate and the places we stayed over the period of this incredible adventure.

Most of the photographs come from the author's collection. Others were donated by the Westbound and Eastbound Crew's personal phones.

To my family, friends, and work colleagues who have supported my writing exploits over the years, giving me the encouragement and motivation needed to get the job done.

Table of Contents

Dedication iii
Acknowledgements v
Introduction ix
Chapter 1 Birth of the Mother Road 1
Chapter 2 The Bucket List 4
Chapter 3 Jockeys and their Steeds 7
Chapter 4 Getting to the Start 14
Chapter 5 Westbound 26
Chapter 6 Eastbound 79
Chapter 7 Post Adventure Wrap Up - Fun Facts and Blog 130

Introduction

I guess this book caught your attention because either you are interested in travelling Route 66 or have already done it and would like to compare notes. Either way, these are two noble reasons to keep reading. I travelled Route 66 with six mates, and I wanted to celebrate the tenth anniversary with a book as a memento of the adventure. Through words and pictures, I hope that you, too, will experience our journey. However, this is not your normal book on Route 66, this is a road trip adventure that uses Route 66 as a guiding light. Any adventure has a start, a middle, and an end. Here, the start was corralling everyone to Chicago for the kick-off. The middle was experiencing Route 66 with a few diversions, and the end was ensuring everyone's safe return home, including me. These front and rear parts can be mini ventures all their own. Throw in a couple of unexpected events along the way and we have a unique Route 66 adventure. Here, a 7,509-mile road trip that crosses dozens of state lines and involved 26 sleepovers; few were in the same bed. So, sit back, buckle up, indulge in a beverage of your choice, and join us for the ride of a lifetime.

Nigel Sainsbury & Route 66, Fairfax, Virginia

Nigel Sainsbury 2024

Chapter 1
Birth of the Mother Road

 Today in the USA, as with other places in the world, most people prefer to get from A to B as quickly as possible. People usually fly within the USA due to long distances between major cities. Americans treat air travel like a public transportation system. Although quicker and often cheaper than other modes of transport, you see little of the real United States from 36,000 feet. The same could be said of the interstate system. The expansive road network connects major towns and cities in the USA, but you miss out on experiencing the authentic America. Huge stretches of these tarmac and concrete superhighways are flanked by unadorned concrete partition walls and tree lines so thick they can obscure your view of the sun.

Before the establishment of the 1956 Interstate Highway Act, the only way to get from A to B was on normal roads, the now-familiar federal highway system. Black and white shields were placed at strategic positions and intersections to mark the correct route. Even number routes run east/west, whilst odd numbers run north/south. As these routes were becoming more popular, they attracted federal funding, but only if they were built and maintained to the required standard. Prior to the idea of these new routes, the only way to navigate across the country was to understand the local and regional auto trails like the Ozark Trail and the Lincoln Highway. These auto trails were not official, and the standard of road surfaces drastically varied. The trails were difficult to navigate because people had to search for colored markings and letters on telegraph poles as guides. Route 66 is a combination of these trails along with existing foot tracks, railroad tracks, and of course, new build roads that joined up the trails and tracks where nothing existed previously – this is most evident from the Midwest to California.

Cars in the late 20s to late 40s were slower and less dependable than modern cars. Knowing how to maintain them was just as important as knowing how to drive. Therefore, road trips took on an adventure all their own. A mixture of concrete and asphalt pathways, Route 66 guides adventurers across 2,448 highway miles, passing through eight of the lower

48 states. From the shoreline of Lake Michigan in Chicago, Illinois, to the pier in Santa Monica, California. The end of the trail sign on the pier was installed in 2009 to mark both the physical and spiritual end to the journey. A distance that could almost take you from the Earth's surface to its core and back, or more realistically, from Edinburgh, Scotland to Istanbul, Turkey. It's a bloody long road. Getting to your holiday destination in the earlier part of the 20th century was just as big a deal as the destination itself and would usually soak up a fair chunk of vacation time.

Before my move to Northern Virginia from New Zealand in 2012, I had only visited the United States a handful of times over my 50+ years. The contiguous *'lower 48'*, as they are colloquially known, covers a land area of over three million square miles, about the size of Australia. But with a population of over 300 million, it dwarfs Aussies population by a factor of ten. The USA is famous for many things like Disney, Ford cars, the Grand Canyon, the Great Lakes, and Yosemite National Park, to name a few. So why is Route 66 just as famous as these American landmarks and brands? After all, it's nothing more than a manmade network of roads; a squiggly line on a road map. That is true, of course, of any route, but Route 66 represents much more than a series of interconnected roads. It was the portal through America. Route 66 was affectionately called *'Main Street of America'* or *'Mother Road'*, two very appropriate names. Essential amenities like gas stations, diners, and motels sprung up along the route, and when built up near natural landmark sites or manmade attractions, the route was all about the journey, less about the destination.

Route 66 brought people together, linked rural communities and became a smorgasbord of food, culture, businesses, and other activities. Entrepreneurs created smart and unique ways to get travellers to stay in their hotels and spend their vacation money on entertainment, food, and lodging. The options were many and businesses thrived on the fruits of the travelling American public.

Established in November 1926 (the year the US introduced the Numbered Highway System), decommissioned in June 1985 and even up to the present day, the 2,448 miles of Route 66 continues to be a traveller's experience, an exploration of America. Through the Great Depression, Route 66 carried people's hopes and dreams of a better life in the west. During World War II, Route 66 supported the quickest way to get military logistics to the Pacific. It has served several purposes over the decades, supporting its nomenclature as the *'Main Street of America.'* During its time as an official route, it witnessed many changes and realignments because of the evolution of the towns it passed through, and the proliferation of bypasses. Today, approximately 80% of Route 66 remains drivable, although not all of it is paved.

If I did nothing else in my three years of living in the United States except ride Route 66 on my motorcycle, I would be happy. That I would have experienced something unique, a road trip that more people dream about than have done it. An adventure where you can stop whenever, and wherever, to soak up the atmosphere and everything the place has to offer. Everyone who knows about American culture and cars has heard of Route 66. It connects the past, present, and future. In 1946, Bobby Troup wrote 'Get Your Kicks' (On Route 66), a popular song made even more famous in the 1960s by Chuck Berry and the Rolling Stones. It's a song that captures the excitement of a road trip with something for everyone.

Back in 2013, Route 66 had already ceased to be a continuous route from start to finish. Segments of the route had either been consumed by superhighways or replaced by alternative roads leaving parts of the old *Mother Road* to deteriorate back to natural form. Some stretches of the road had been disregarded because they were no longer fit for normal traffic. As we age, parts of our body change and we look a little different, too. Well, Route 66 has suffered a similar fate over the years, but that doesn't mean that it has lost any of its spirit and character - and it hasn't. The American culture and appetite for cars, travel, food, and entertainment were as much alive in 2013 as they would have been back in the 30s, 40s and 50s. Although not as active in 2013, we still got to experience much of what Route 66 offers and will cherish the memories for a very long time to come.

Chapter 2
The Bucket List

When I moved my family to New Zealand in 2004 to start a new career with the Royal New Zealand Air Force (RNZAF), I never thought for a moment that I would end up concluding my career in the USA some 12 years later. I was assigned to the New Zealand Embassy in Washington, DC, as the Air Attaché to the USA and Defence Advisor to Canada. Initially, I thought I would only be there for the standard three-year appointment. What I never factored into the equation was meeting a beautiful American woman who would say *'Yes'* to marriage. So here I am, 11 years later (2023), living the dream!

However, let's not get ahead of ourselves here. We need to roll the clock back to mid-2012 when I found out that I was going to the USA. I had never made up a bucket list of things to do during a posting, but I realized that this was an opportunity to change that. Number one on the list was going to be riding the iconic Route 66 on a motorcycle. Number two on the list was getting a motorcycle to do it on. The other 20-plus experiences that got added to the list over the coming months also seemed to be centred on motorcycles. So, I quickly realised that I needed a larger bucket. I saw the *'bucket list'* as a metaphor for the opportunities that would come my way during this tour. The following three years would be packed with excitement.

My predecessors warned I would need to plan any major holidays as soon as I arrived in Washington, DC, and well before I had got myself into any work routine. Several friends who were interested in Route 66 asked to stay updated on my progress. So, with a clear mission and a vision of what it might look like, on arrival in the USA in November 2012, I set about planning a trip of a lifetime. The *'Kiwi Route 66 Adventure'* would become a reality less than a year later.

When you take up a new position, there is usually a *'honeymoon period'* where things are quieter until you get accustomed to the workload and its tempo. I knew this period would be the best time to get this #1 bucket list item sorted. All the others would be more flexible, including #2 on the list, which was to purchase a motorcycle to take back to New Zealand. Clearly, #2 would leap up to the #1 slot once I had settled into my new routine. All the other things on the list would seamlessly dovetail into my work schedule.

By the time I had settled into my new apartment in Arlington, Virginia, getting a bike had become an obsession. I logged onto the computer in the business centre of the apartment block one night and found precisely what I was searching for, or rather, it found me.

Not being an American, I thought everyone in the USA who was serious about motorcycles rode a Harley Davidson. Not true, of course. I am generalising a bit here to frame how I was thinking. But there are a hell of a lot of Harley's in the USA. Every major city seems to have a Harley Davidson dealership. Although Route 66 is an American experience, I didn't feel the need to do the trip on a Harley. I had owned a Sportster in New Zealand for a few years, and I wanted something different. It would be my one bike for all occasions whilst in the USA.

My criteria for the Google search were straightforward. I didn't want a Harley or anything that looked like a Harley. I also didn't want it to be a dual sport adventure bike like my BMW R 1200 GS back home. However, it had to be big enough to eat up huge mileages and have enough luggage capacity to get me through being on the road for a few weeks. My intention was to travel extensively around the United States on this bike. It also had to be small enough for local jaunts and the daily commute to the embassy when the weather was favourable. Finally, after three years, I would want to take this bike back home to New Zealand as a keepsake and partner for my BMW R 1200 GS. A perfect two-bike stable for entering semi-retirement. I had set myself a budget of $8000.

As tight as my criteria seemed, after a few clicks of the mouse, the computer search presented me with the perfect bike. A bright red 2007, 1100 cc, Air Cooled, V-Twin, Moto Guzzi, Griso, which came with a Moto Guzzi four-piece luggage set. It was perfect. It was well within budget at $6000 and located a mere four hundred miles up the road

2007 Moto Guzzi Griso & New Zealand Embassy, Washington DC.

in a dealership in Boston, Massachusetts. I would pick up the bike in early 2013. That was an adventure all of itself and is detailed in my book *'One Down Four Up–My Bikes, My Life.'*

From the get-go, I never wanted this to be a solo adventure. Although motorcycle riding is usually done alone, it's more fun to do it with friends who enjoy it too. Shared experiences are just the best. What I had given no thought to was finding myself a motorcycling buddy. But that opportunity found me in a local pub on Christmas Eve 2012.

I had been in the USA for just three weeks and found myself alone in my apartment watching TV, wondering what to do. Christmas can be a very lonely time when you don't have kids and other family members around you. I didn't want my first Christmas in the USA to be lonely, so I dressed up and headed out to find a pub. Unlike the UK or New Zealand, where everything would have been open, it seemed the opposite was true. The first pub I found open was called the Liberty Tavern. The crowd was just right, not too packed to drown out the background music, and I easily found an empty stool at the bar. Once seated, I instinctively struck up a conversation with a friendly couple sitting next to me who were moving to Italy for work. As is usual during conversations, motorbikes cropped up, and I mentioned I had a BMW R 1200 GS at home in New Zealand. The words BMW R1200 GS got the attention of a chap to the side of me at the bar who looked across and was taking notice. His reaction was like someone had just called out his name.

A short while afterwards, the couple I was chatting with left the pub and the chap who heard me mentioning the BMW leaned across the bar and asked me about my bike. He introduced himself as Alex, and he was with his girlfriend Sarah. Turns out Alex also had a BMW R1200 GS, but the slightly larger Adventure model. While we were talking, I told Alex about my bucket list. I said that my top priority was to ride Route 66 with some friends from New Zealand in 2013. I asked Alex if he was interested in coming along. I had barely finished my sentence before he chirped in and said, *'Yep, I'm in'*. That was the start of a bromance that endures to this day.

I was off to a successful start. Within three weeks of arriving in the states, I had found myself a beautiful Italian motorcycle and a motorcycling buddy who was as keen as me to ride Route 66.

Chapter 3
Jockeys and their Steeds

Back in New Zealand, my mate Adrian *'Sid'* Collins was the strongest advocate for supporting a Route 66 adventure and was the first to sign up to the idea. However, Sid had a plan of his own. He wanted to visit the Barber Motorcycle Museum in Alabama, the Jack Daniel Distillery in Tennessee, and attend the World of Speed event at Bonneville Salt Flats in Utah in early September. Sid didn't do too well in his geography lessons at school, as none of these venues are in states that were even close to Route 66. That was challenge number one. The second challenge was that Sid needed a motorcycle.

Like me, Sid had also served in the RAF and had transitioned to New Zealand back in the 1990s. We had crossed paths in the RAF and worked together in the RNZAF, so we had been mates for years. I had also trusted Sid with the guardianship of my treasured BMW R1200 GS whilst I was living in the USA. So, no greater confidence in a mate than to trust him with your two-wheeled baby. Sid, who is a skilled motorcycle mechanic, felt at ease riding a used motorcycle and left it to me to select the right one.

British people are inherently frugal, and Sid's plan was simple. Buy a cheap bike, use it, then sell it - done. The option of buying and then selling rather than renting over several weeks is a much cheaper option than renting over the same period. So,

Vintage (1986) Kawasaki Concurs 1000, New Zealand Embassy, Washington DC.

my challenge was to find such a bike.

Cycle Trader, eBay, Auto Trader and Craigs List are all excellent sites for second-hand motorcycles in the USA. It took me a while to scan all these sites and filter the searches because there are thousands of bikes for sale at any one time. I didn't know what I was looking for, nor did I have much of an idea of what *'cheap'* was. I kept the search to a radius of 25 miles, thinking I could easily pick it up or have the owner deliver it to me. In my head, I thought that working with a budget of around $2000 would get me something to do the job. That then highlighted a few other financial considerations. Registration, insurance, and storage.

As a diplomat, any motor vehicle I owned had to be declared to the Office of Foreign Missions (OFM) which is part of the Department of State. In declaring this to be my vehicle, it would need to display a diplomatic tag, otherwise known as a number plate, and I would have to surrender the title to the OFM. Bugger. That would mean I would have to buy and sell the bike myself. And if Sid was riding it one way to the end of Route 66, it would be stuck thousands of miles away from me. With no immediate answer to this dilemma, a perfect solution was about to land in my lap in just a few weeks, which would make the trip even cheaper for Sid.

I lived in an apartment block that had no spare space for additional vehicles. So, I needed to find a secondary storage place for the bike. I used my new diplomatic skills to chat with the facilities manager at the embassy about my upcoming Route 66 adventure during a Friday night happy hour. Having piqued her interest, I floated the idea of storing a spare motorcycle in the underground carpark of the embassy. I suggested the bike was small enough to be parked next to the heating or air conditioning systems without taking up a car parking space. It worked; permission granted.

The bike I ended up purchasing was a 1986 first generation Kawasaki Concours, with about a million miles on it. It was well used. I got the price down to $1200 from $1500, which was well within my *'cheap'* budget. The bike's built-in luggage, protective fairing, top box, and high windshield made it an excellent choice for the trip, but it was too large to hide in the embassy. The tough part of the story was not dealing with the embassy management, although that was challenging enough. It was purchasing the bike. I wanted to see the bike in the flesh before I bought it. It was for sale in the south-eastern part of Washington, DC, an area not known for its friendliness, and not a place for me to be alone on foot, in the dark on a cold February evening.

I waited 15 minutes for the seller, who arrived just as my anxiety levels were peaking. He arrived outside the house we agreed to meet at. Not sure that he lived there, but he seemed honest enough and we swiftly made the deal so I could get the hell out of there and bring my anxiety level down a few notches.

He delivered the bike to me at the embassy a few days later as we had arranged. I hid the bike in the embassy's underground car park before registering it as a diplomatic vehicle. But it ended up taking more space than I expected, and the facilities manager called me in. I apologised for my miscalculation, but she wasn't happy with me or my excuses. I had clearly taken advantage of her good nature, and she reminded me of that fact. But there was more to come just a few months later, and that would really piss her off.

Sid had planned to be in the USA for about a month and had been lobbying a couple of other mates who had also shown an interest in the Kiwi Route 66 Adventure. The first was his neighbour and friend, Neil Surtees or 'Surtz'. Surtz is a fascinating chap who can make and fix just about anything with his hands. He made his mark by designing and building fishing boats. His logo is "*Surtees Boats - Built to Fish.*" It's a well-known brand amongst fishermen in New Zealand (which equates to about 80% of the population). His boats are famous both in New Zealand and across the Tasman Sea in Australia. Surtz also builds and often races custom cars because he can. But his other passion is motorcycles. Surtz saw a chance to purchase a Harley Davidson from the USA, ride across Route 66, and ship it back to New Zealand after Sid outlined his plan. However, storing another bike at the embassy would create problems for Nigel with the facility's manager.

Harley Road King, New Zealand Eembassy, Washington, DC.

Surtz did his research and secured an agreement on a Harley Davidson Road King from a dealer in Tampa, Florida. Once again, registration and storage were two immediate problems that had to be resolved.

I arranged for the bike to be delivered to the embassy and requested the registration papers be sent by post just before Surtz' arrival. Figuring the dealership could issue a temporary registration tag for 30 days allowing Surtz to ride for the duration he was in the USA. Then we would simply load the bike into a container in Los Angeles and ship it to New Zealand.

I gave the nice facilities manager at the embassy a serious listening to about my taking advantage of her considerate nature. After my sheepish apology and sad face, she softened a little and then reluctantly agreed to let me store the Harley next to the Kawasaki. After all, it would not take up another car parking space – would it? When I rode my Guzzi to work, the lower-level garage looked more like a motorcycle showroom than an embassy car park, but I was not quite done yet!

The other mate that Sid was lobbying was also an RNZAF mate. Brett Shanks, or *'Shag'* as he was affectionately known. Like Surtz, Shag also saw the opportunity to do something special. Shag was a big bike lover even though he was built like the scarecrow out of The Wizard of Oz. Shag bought one of the biggest bikes on the planet, a Honda Valkyrie. This thing was enormous and weighed in at well over 700 lbs and was as big as a car.

Shag purchased it from a chap called Bob Smith, in Tulsa, Oklahoma. Bob is one of the few people in the world that specializes in Honda Valkyries and his craftmanship speaks for itself. Between Bob, Shag and myself, we got the logistics sorted. The registration and insurance were much easier this time. Bob would leave the tag on the bike and insure it for Shag. When the trip was complete, Shag would send the tag back to Bob once the bike had been safely loaded into the container alongside Surtz' Harley.

Arranging local storage at the embassy for this

Honda Valkyrie, New Zealand Embassy, Washington, DC.

Route 66 – A Guiding Light

behemoth of a bike was always going to be challenging. I was shitting myself just thinking about asking the facility manager a third time. Not only that, but this time I would absolutely need a full car parking space. The conversation did not go well. The facility's manager was pissed off beyond belief and berated me for abusing my embassy privilege. She said she would have to limit access to other embassy staff in allowing this. I had no defense and had run out of apologies and positive things to say to her. I kept expressing gratitude for her help and support whilst guaranteeing that the three bikes would be gone in a few weeks. It didn't help my case much when the facilities manager (plus a few others) saw this fucking colossal motorcycle being manhandled off the back of a U-Haul truck by three large 250lb+ gentlemen right outside the main entrance of the embassy. The embassy's underground garage now looked like a motorcycle auction room, and my colleagues were not happy with me.

We now had a gang of five; me on an Italian Moto Guzzi, Alex on a German BMW, Sid on a Japanese Kawasaki, Surtz on an all-American Harley and Shag riding his 700lb+ slab of Japanese engineering wrapped up under the disguise of a Honda Valkyrie. We would be the Westbound Crew of five.

I first met Padre Paul Allen-Baines when I was the Commanding Officer of the RNZAF Ground Training School back in 2008. Paul was an RNZAF Chaplin, and with all the other support services, provided pastoral care to the trainees and staff. Paul was also an avid motorcyclist. During our time working together, we had become friends and shared several adventures on motorcycles all over New Zealand. Paul was married to Pam; an American from Illinois, and I thought it would be a great opportunity for them both to be involved in this adventure. Paul was very keen, Pam not so much, but was very supportive of Paul having an adventure with a couple of mates. Paul also had a friend who was interested in riding Route 66. His name was Ian Davidson. I had never met Ian, but a mate of Paul's was a mate of mine. We now had a crew of seven.

We all struggled with taking time off work and, naturally, financing the trip, although it was a little easier and cheaper for Alex and me. To come from New Zealand, travel for three weeks plus, and stay in hotels was a financial balancing act. Everyone was still employed, so all our schedules differed. For Paul and Ian, their time was restricted, and then it occurred to me we could split the adventure in two. Alex and I had to do the journey twice anyway, or else we would have to ship the bikes back by road transportation once we had completed the Westbound Adventure.

The start and finish for Alex and me was always going to be Arlington. Sid had planned on being away from home for a month and, as luck would have it, both Surtz and Shag aligned with Sid. Indeed, Shag would have a somewhat extended holiday for a special occasion on the West Coast which only Shag knew about. What this meant was by finishing in Santa Monica, Paul, and Ian could fly into LAX and then ride Eastbound with Alex and me. Not only that, but Paul could ride the Kawasaki back so I could sell it back home in Virginia; perfect. The upfront cost of the bike and resale could then be split between Sid and Paul, making the trip for both much cheaper than any other option. Ian was more traditional and had decided that the only way to do Route 66 was on a Harley, so he booked a one-way rental from California to Chicago. With a name like Davidson, you could *Harley* blame him for wanting to do the trip on a local bike.

With the logistics sorted for the bikes, and the dates for World of Speed locked in, we now had the rough outline of a plan and a timeline for this whole adventure. Well, sort of…we still didn't know when we would start and did not know when it would finish. But those details would get thrashed out closer to the time and once Sid, Surtz, and Shag had locked in their flights. As all three had single syllable names beginning with the letter 'S', I refer to them as '*S Cubed*' or simply '*S3*'' throughout the book, just to keep things concise.

There was a fair bit of responsibility resting on my shoulders here, but what the hell, it was going to be quite an adventure for us all. The more tasks I had to do, the more my enthusiasm for this whole thing grew. I had sorted three different bikes by three different means, stored them and had a plan to ensure they would be street-legal for the period they were being used. I also gave some thought to recording and capturing the adventure so people could follow us. I got a GoPro 3 camera to mount on my Moto Guzzi and would use my Olympus compact camera at other times. I also set up a daily blog site on the picasaweb.google.com public site so that loved ones and mates could follow along and make comments. In hindsight, I should have just started a Facebook page, but in my defense, I was new to all this social media stuff.

My little two-bedroom apartment in Arlington could comfortably accommodate S3 with a couple of blow-up beds. This would keep accommodation costs for them to a minimum. Now we just needed to put a little more detail on this Route 66 adventure.

I had also promised to accommodate a couple of special cuddly friends as passengers. A stuffed Welsh Dragon and a Kiwi bird. The Dragon was gifted to me by a special school friend who had a terminal illness back in 2010. Sian Evans had been like a sister to me growing up and I had promised her that the Dragon would accompany me on my travels—wherever they took me. The Kiwi came along as company for the Dragon. Sadly, Sian passed away in March 2012, aged just 51, but not before I sent a load of pictures back to Sian of me, my motorcycle, and the Red Dragon from all over New Zealand. I went back to the UK in August 2012 to pay my respects. Her ashes had been scattered up the dingle, a wooded area where we used to play as kids. The Red Dragon accompanied me on that day, too. It was the first time I had lost a childhood friend the same age as me and it made me reflect on how short our lives really are. I wept a lot that day.

The Red Dragon was then, and still is today, a constant reminder of what life is all about and how we should make the most of the one life we know of. This adventure would

Welsh Dragon and Kiwi Bird, Cuyama Highway, California

be the last time the Red Dragon would accompany me on my travels. That would be some 18 months after Sian had passed away. The Dragon and the Kiwi now sit on my bookcase overlooking my home office. Their travelling days over.

Chapter 4
Getting to the Start

It wasn't hard to figure out that if World of Speed in Utah was over the weekend of the 7th and 8th of September, we would need to start our Westbound adventure around the end of August. At this time of year, the weather and temperature would be perfect for motorcycling, kids would be back in school, summer traffic would be less, and accommodation easier to secure. Realistically, we were looking to ride between five and eight hours a day at an average speed of around 45 mph, so that would give us a range of between 225 and 360 miles a day.

We estimated the trip from Virginia to Chicago to Los Angeles and back to Virginia (without deviations) would take three weeks and cover 5,500 miles. However, there would be some serious deviations to those assumptions, so we added another week for luck. This rough outline would be enough information to book time off work and inform others in New Zealand. The assumptions turned out to be quite close. The actual dates were 29th August through 23rd September.

Of us all, Sid was the one who wanted to get a little more out of the trip than just Route 66. I was happy with whatever we decided. Alex and I would experience the Route 66 bits we missed going west on the Eastbound leg coming home. Adding the southern states to the overall adventure was difficult for Alex and me because of work

Westbound Crew Meet & Greet, Nigel, Sid, Shag, Alex & Surtz, Arlington, Virginia

schedules, but we all thought the World of Speed would be a fun stop on the Westbound adventure.

S3 arrived on August 22nd, and we immediately headed off to a speed dating event at the embassy to introduce everyone to their motorcycles. I thought it would be best to avoid introducing them to the facilities manager. They didn't need to be subjected to the comments I had received. My thinking was that she would just be grateful that the bikes were finally gone. So, to avoid any skirmish, I stealthily sneaked everyone into the underground garage of the embassy, and once everyone had made their acquaintances with the bikes, we wasted no time in leaving and headed straight back to my apartment in Arlington. That night, Alex came over to meet S3 and celebrate the gathering of the Westbound Crew. We started the Route 66 adventure by having beer and pizza and talking about our hopes and expectations.

Westbound Crew, Apartment Basement, Arlington, Virginia

S3 wanted to visit the southern states and explore the Barber Motorcycle Museum in Alabama, as well as the Jack Daniel Distillery and Nashville music scene in Tennessee. Doing that from Virginia before embarking on Route 66 was an easy pre-start adventure. I had sourced a gigantic map of the USA so we could draw the route we wanted to take whilst trying to fit in all the different places everyone wanted to visit. Considering S3 was heading to Chicago from the south and Alex and I from the east, we picked Indianapolis as an intersection point. We agreed to gather in Indianapolis on the night of Friday, August 30th, 2013. That would be a great place to start the Westbound adventure. Then we could all ride into Chicago sometime on Saturday 31st, find the start point of Route 66 and get the main event underway.

THURSDAY 29TH AUGUST
DESTINATION CLARKSBURG, WV.

I knew that S3 had ticked all the boxes of their mini adventure down south because Sid rang me at 11 pm Wednesday night to tell me. He didn't need to mention that they had made it to a bar in Nashville and were enjoying the live music because his voice was drowned out by the Country & Western howling going on in the background. I think he must have been standing right next to a loudspeaker, just in case I didn't believe him. He said that they had made a pit stop at a Honda dealership and Shag added about another 100lbs of bling and accessories to his already overweight Honda Valkyrie. On the positive side, the additional weight would help Shag build up the muscle group in his spindly legs. I thanked Sid for his timely, considerate call, reminding him that Alex and I were starting our own mini warm-up adventure in just seven hours.

Alex and Me, Harley Davidson Factory, York, Pennsylvania

I am not sure why Alex and I had planned a Harley Davidson factory tour on the same day we were starting our cross-country adventure — but we did. This small 220-mile round car trip to York, Pennsylvania, was ambitious, to say the least. The thought that we could just *'nip up'* to York, do a factory tour and then *'nip back'* to Arlington before climbing on our motorcycles and heading west was insane. Our saving grace was that Alex had a Porsche 911 *'time machine'* so the 110-mile trip back to Arlington could be covered in no time at all if we really needed to. Turns out we needed all the horses the Porsche could give us. We left at 06:30 am and arrived at the Harley factory well ahead of the

09:30 am start time for the tour. This was the second time Alex and I had done this tour. Just three weeks beforehand, on Saturday 3rd August, we had been lucky enough to get a personalised (behind the scenes) tour by the General Manager, Ed Magee. To do a public tour after a personal tour by the GM would be a tall ask; and it was. The public tour didn't even come a close second and fell short of expectations. The story of how we got the personal tour is worth recounting because it was entirely by chance.

Alex and I had been out for a ride one Saturday afternoon and, as is normal, we called into our local pub, sat outside with a cold beer, and debriefed the ride. Sitting at a table next to us were two blokes happily having a conversation, but they overheard Alex and I talking about bikes. One of them mentioned that their friend, Ed Magee, works as the General Manager of the Harley Davidson factory in York, Pennsylvania, and offered to introduce us to him. We chatted a little more and then he picked up his phone and rang Ed. After pleasantries had been exchanged, he introduced me and passed the phone over. I chatted with Ed and apologized for how this conversation had come about. Ed generously offered to arrange a private factory tour for us instead of a group tour with strangers, trusting his friend's opinion of Alex and me. And that is how we got to see how Harleys were made for the first time. Pure luck by being in the right place at the right time.

Alex, myself, and another mate of Alex's arrived at the factory early on a Saturday morning on our motorcycles, none of which were Harleys. This was not lost on the smart but casually dressed guy who came out to greet us. He introduced himself as Ed Magee, the man on the

Alex and Me Harley Davidson Factory Tour, York, Pennsylvania

phone. Turns out that Ed had served 15 years in the Marine Corps, so we had the military connection right away. Ed showed us around everywhere, even the parts of the factory where the public could not go. It was unbelievable. He knew about all the motorcycle models made at the factory, including Softail, Touring, Tri-Glide, and Custom Vehicle Operations (CVO). He described all the specialist processes and the entire logistics chain for making Harley-Davidson a global brand. I found it all fascinating, especially the global logistics of creating, storing, and distributing next year's models while keeping them firmly under wraps. Ed had led a lean transformation program of manufacturing operations, and the results were impressive. Ed explained the process of getting new bike models ready for release and how they implemented production changes. We had a tremendous time, and he made the public tour look lame in comparison.

The second (public) tour was an opportunity for me to take a couple of bottles of our best New Zealand, Marlborough, Sauvignon Blanc wine as a thank-you to Ed for his time. We never saw Ed the second time but left the wine and a thank you note with his staff and headed back to start our Route 66 adventure. As we headed back home, we got caught in some heavy slow-moving traffic because of a major road closure which we never saw on the GPS. This resulted in us backtracking a little before Alex put the Porsche through its paces on the back roads of Pennsylvania and Maryland to get us home. We were 90 minutes late getting back, which is not a big problem usually, but we were about to start a three-

Alex and Me Outside Apartment, Arlington, Virginia

week motorcycle adventure, which put us under pressure from the beginning.

We had agreed to meet up with S3 in Indianapolis on Friday 30th August, so we had some serious riding to do if we were going to achieve that. The day had started at 6:30 am. We drove to York and back, packed our bikes, and rode for almost five and a half hours, covering 250 miles. We arrived at our first overnight destination in Clarksburg, West Virginia, at 9:30 pm. It had been dark for a while, and we were both exhausted but got within 50 miles of our halfway target, so not a bad recovery.

The BMW and Guzzi, Monongahela National Forest, West Virginia

We could have comfortably taken the Interstate Road to make up the time, but that was not what this adventure was about. This trip was all about the journey, not the destination. We would get there eventually. We enjoyed a pleasant day with dry, slightly cloudy skies and a temperature of 92F. The twisty roads guiding us through the Appalachian Mountains and the Monongahela National Forest delivered an outstanding riding experience for the first day. The fresh countryside air blowing down the inside of my visor carried the multiple rural fragrances you just don't experience when riding in a city or driving in a car. My brain was in overload, trying to differentiate the multitude of smells. I felt the whole day had been a tremendous privilege. Riding at a slower pace than normal was high on my agenda today, and I was particularly focussed going around corners because I didn't know how my luggage would affect the handling characteristics of the bike. I needn't have worried. With the tires nice and warm and sticky, the Moto Guzzi soaked up the bends with ease and was just as eager as me to get to the next one. I thought to myself during those moments that this was going to be one great adventure.

FRIDAY 30TH AUGUST
DESTINATION INDIANAPOLIS, IL.

S3 had arrived early in Indianapolis and spent most of the day at the Top Fuel Dragsters event before chilling out downtown, waiting for Alex and me to arrive. We had left Clarksburg around 9:00 am and set off along Route 50, knowing that we had a long day ahead of us. The fine and warm weather set the tone for a great riding day.

Alex 'No Helmet' State Line West Virgina & Ohio

We were both excited to get going and meet up with S3. After about 90 minutes of riding, we crossed over the Ohio river near Parkersburg, West Virginia into Ohio. This crossing was our fourth state line crossing. We began in Virginia and went through West Virginia near Wardensville. Then we briefly crossed into Maryland near Mt Storm and returned to West Virginia near Redhouse.

We had travelled less than a mile into Ohio when Alex pulled over, dismounted his bike, removed his helmet and smiled at me. *"What the fuck are you doing?"* I asked. Alex just laughed. Ohio is one of several states that allows you to ride without a helmet providing you are over the age of 18. Wearing a helmet saved my life back in 1979, but just for shits and giggles, I too rode without a helmet – but just for a few miles. I did not enjoy the experience. All sorts of crap flew into my face, and I just didn't feel comfortable, so the helmet went straight back on again.

Interestingly, the number of Harley Davidson dealerships in the USA had reached 675 in 2023. Indeed, only the District of Columbia within the lower 48 states is without one. Even Chillicothe, a small township in Ohio, has a dealership. I know this because we stopped there for a break. Pulling up on a BMW R1200 GS and a Moto Guzzi Griso would never win over any hearts and minds. Nevertheless, they presented an excellent chance to exchange stories over a cup of coffee with the staff, who were polite and friendly.

A broken down truck in Cincinnati caused a minor setback, resulting in a 30-minute delay to our arrival in Indianapolis. We eventually got to the hotel around 7 pm. We had covered 403 miles in eight hours and one minute.

Our crossing into Indiana at West Harrison was state line crossing #5. I was still upskilling myself on using the GoPro whilst riding, but I had

Nigel 'No Helmet' Chillicothe, Ohio

become adept at taking hands-free photos with my little Olympus compact camera. Many of those photos are in this book. Our arrival in Indianapolis and meeting up with S3 was a great feeling, and I felt we were firmly back on track. The beer was cold, the company warm, and everything we had planned and talked about had led us to this moment. It was a tremendous end to the day. We spent the next few hours drinking beer and exchanging experiences from our mini-prestart adventures. We were all looking forward to tomorrow. That would be the start of the main event, mile zero of Route 66. An early morning kick stands up was on the cards.

Route 66 – A Guiding Light

ROUTE 66 START DAY, SATURDAY 31ST AUGUST DESTINATION PONTIAC, IL.

Today was the first time all five of us had ridden together as the Westbound Crew. S3 had been riding as a group for a week. Alex and I had been riding together for over six months, but from the get-go on this first morning, the group of five just seemed to gel.

We left the hotel at Indianapolis nice and early, at 08:40am. The day was perfect for riding. We briefly paused for a group photo at the Indianapolis Motor Speedway, where Indy 500 and NASCAR races are held, before setting off towards Chicago.

Shag & Alex, Gas Station, Hammond, Indiana

However, the nice day would not last. As we were approaching Chicago, we hit our first batch of inclement weather in Hammond. The spectacular lightning show was accompanied by thunderclaps so loud and local; you could feel them reverberate through your body. We were sitting ducks on motorcycles.

We immediately took refuge at a gas station (what the hell were we thinking!!) and waited for the storm to pass. The rain hammered down so intensely that it bounced off the ground as if it were rubber. The sheer volume of water was choking up the storm drains, causing local flash flooding everywhere. Then, just when we thought we would be ok, and with only 20 miles to run into Chicago, we were convinced we would beat the next storm coming up behind us. Sadly, we were badly mistaken. We had quickly found cover from the first storm. But the rain gods were just playing with us. This time, they timed the downpour perfectly and hit us whilst we were out in the open with no immediate cover. Again, the downpour was so intense that we got completely soaked. It was like being hosed down by a fire truck. This was the first of several drenchings we would experience on this adventure. Another necessary unscheduled stop (again in the safety of a gas station) forced a change of clothes and a rethink about where we could realistically get to after we had found the start of Route 66.

West Bound Crew, Shag, Nigel, Sid, Surtz & Alex, East Adams Street, Chicago, Illinois

You meet some truly nice people at gas stations. Customers were curious about our unique accents and non-Harley motorcycles, wanting to know more about us, our bikes, and our adventure. A few of them shared their own stories about Route 66 whilst making some recommendations on things to see and do along the way.

Once the weather front had finally passed, we had a clear run into Chicago. We were so eager to get there that we missed the starting point and spent almost 30 minutes looking for the tiny sign that marks the beginning of the *Mother Road*. In my mind, I was expecting to find a huge fuck off sign with flashing lights and bright colours; something so obvious it couldn't be missed. It was a little disappointing then to find this farty little brown historic Route 66 sign on a spindly black post stuck on the sidewalk on the corner of East Adams St. and South Michigan Ave. On reflection, I was surprised that I never actually researched the start point; I had spent so much time and effort on getting things sorted for the whole adventure that these smaller details didn't feature on my list of things to do. In a way, that was a good thing, because the entire experience of driving around Chicago trying to find the start sign was a lot of fun. We later discovered that the actual start of Route 66 was closer to the lake, about ½ mile away from where we initially thought.

Alex and I mused we would be back at this same road sign in just a few weeks' time. We didn't know it then, but this would be the only time we would see this sign. Our plans would change big time during our Eastbound adventure and something quite different would happen.

We took some cheesy photos and congratulated each other on reaching the start before leaving at 3:45 pm Central Standard Time (CST). Only then did we realise we had entered CST (gained an hour) just after leaving Indianapolis. Alex and I had travelled 863 miles in three days to get here, and S3 around 1,500 miles over a week.

Wienermobile, Pontiac, Illinois

People typically travel Route 66 from east to west. Indeed, the Lewis and Clark expedition in the 1800s was all about a westward expansion of the United States, but they never had Route 66 to guide them like us. Chicago, St. Louis, and Los Angeles are the three largest cities along Route 66. The common denominator being their ability to supply water. Again, a throwback to the Lewis and Clark days. Travelling west through different time zones and gaining an hour each time is far easier on the body clock. The opposite would be true, of course, coming back east.

The gentle ride out of the city was on Interstate 55, parts of which is still recognised as Route 66. We arrived in Pontiac, Illinois after a changeable, but enjoyable day, having travelled some 311 miles in exactly seven hours. As we pulled into our hotel, we spotted an Oscar Mayer Wienermobile, a contraption that looks like a tumescent penis on wheels pretending to look like a hot dog in a bun. Another classic icon of the 50s and a rare sight in 2013.

Nigel & Shag, Pontiac, Illinois

The short two-minute ride to the restaurant with no helmets, gloves or jackets felt completely liberating this time, and like Ohio, is perfectly legal in Illinois. A hearty meal washed down with a couple of cold draft beers is the perfect end to the day. The fun and laughter involved in debriefing such a diverse day with your riding mates is an immensely positive feeling and is extremely motivating for the days to come. Shag and I also enjoyed the challenge of climbing on to the seven-foot fibreglass bull in the parking lot of the steak restaurant, just because we could. It practically begged us to be climbed on. These almost childlike activities fuel the excitement of knowing that we would do it all again tomorrow! This is exactly the type of adventure I had hoped it would be.

Chapter 5
Westbound

In a perfect world, each chapter of a book covers a different section of the overall story, and this book is no different. However, yesterday was the prestart, start, and a bit of the Westbound section all rolled into one. So, this chapter draws a line under all that and starts with the first day that we moved as the Westbound Crew heading towards California. By having this introductory paragraph, it also allowed me to standardize the format of the book. Otherwise, my editor would have had a fit and changed it.

DAY 2, SUNDAY 1ST SEPTEMBER
DESTINATION ROLLA, MO

Who knew that Pontiac, Illinois had one of the best Route 66 museums along The *Mother Road*? I had done minimal research on things to see and do along the route, but I had completely missed this one. I knew we couldn't see everything on Route 66 in a couple of weeks. The ride was to soak up whatever Route 66 had to give us in the moment we were there. I don't even remember how we found the museum; it wasn't a planned stop, but we were all chuffed that we did. An early start from the hotel got us to the museum well before

Route 66 Museum, Shag, Nigel, Surtz, Sid & Alex, Pontiac, Illinois

opening time, so we were restricted to peeping through the window. Then, as we were debating whether we should wait or just get going, Rose, one of the museum curators, opened the doors early and invited us in to look around.

We spent an hour in the museum, and it was well worth it.

Sid the Mechanic, Pontiac, Illinois

We were completely overwhelmed with the stuff that made Route 66 famous. It was a trip back in time and to do this at the start of our adventure just inspired us all to get back on the bikes and get on with it. Anyone visiting this museum would have had a similar motivational experience. The museum had one last surprise for us, and it created (for me anyway) one of the most memorable photographs of the whole adventure. At the back of the museum was a massive wall mural depicting Route 66 and Pontiac, Illinois. Rose took a cool photo of the Westbound Crew with our trusted steeds.

Westbound Crew, Alex, Sid, Shag, Surtz & Nigel, Pontiac, Illinois

The route allowing us to get back onto the *Mother Road* was well signposted from Pontiac and with Alex's keen eye for navigation; we travelled through some quaint towns, each with its own record and specific

Westbound Crew, Sid, Shag, Alex, Couple of Locals, Surtz & Nigel, Atlanta, Illinois

memories of Route 66. In all the times Alex and I had ridden together, I never had to worry about which way was next. I just trusted him and had done so from day one. Alex had a riding buddy and enjoyed the navigation, and I had a mate I was happy to follow. This arrangement allowed me to take in much of the scenery on our rides. The situation here was very similar. Alex led, and we all followed.

We missed some heavy rain on our way to Missouri, but we wouldn't be so lucky a few days later when we had to change our plans because of a serious soaking. We stopped in Atlanta, Illinois for some brunch at a typical 1950s cafe where even the wait staff was dressed in the 1950s period clothing. With the nostalgic 1950s music playing in the background and the authentic surroundings from that era, it felt as if we were transported to the film set of *Back to the Future*. The experience was pretty special. Then we walked through a couple of memorabilia shops. If we thought the museum in Pontiac was a little overwhelming, then these shops were the museum on cocaine. They were stacked from floor to ceiling of Route 66 shit. I mean that in the nicest possible way, but you couldn't distinguish the crap from the good stuff by sight alone. It was visual overload. Route 66 nick-knacks and 1930s to 1960s memorabilia like we had never seen before, even in pictures. Route 66 stamped on it all - posters, records, plastic dolls, tags (number plates), hub caps, toy trains, gas pumps, pens, ashtrays, and more.

One of the most iconic landmarks associated with the love of automobiles was Muffler Man. These statues stood over 20 feet in height and could be found all over America, not just on Route 66, and advertised automotive muffler shops. Several statues had been modified over the years and the one

Hotdog Man & Nigel, Atlanta, Illinois

we found in Atlanta had been moved from the Bunyon's hot dog establishment in Cicero. Guessing where he came from was easy, given that he held a massive seven-foot-long hotdog (with mustard)! Even in 2013, many people in these small towns rely on the passing tourist for their trade, and we were pleased to oblige. We all felt privileged to have met some of these folk who keep the spirit of Route 66 alive for people like us to enjoy.

We passed through Springfield, Illinois, on our way to St. Louis. Every time I think of Springfield, I think of the Simpsons and the antics of Homer and his family. Like Route 66, the Simpsons are iconic symbols of America. At least 34 states have a Springfield, and within two days, we would pass through two of them: Illinois' Springfield and Springfield Missouri. Alex picked up a passenger as we were heading out of Springfield, and not one of us noticed, including Alex. This unwelcome passenger was a bumblebee which somehow got itself trapped in the sleeve of Alex's sweatshirt. Alex surprised us by stopping his bike abruptly, dismounting, and performing an Irish jig while singing out loud. We never saw the bumblebee but had no reason to doubt Alex's story.

As we approached St Louis, we could see the iconic Gateway Arch from about seven miles out. This man-made structure on the

Surtz & Alex 'The Waspman', Springfield, Illinois

banks of the Mississippi River is an awe-inspiring sight. It becomes a very imposing structure the closer you get. The engineering masterpiece was finished in 1965 and stands 630 feet tall, and 630 feet wide, making it the tallest monument in the US. An optical illusion makes it look taller than its width. It has internal elevator trams that swivel while moving through the hoop-like structure. We never had time to ride the trams, so we could only imagine what the view at the top of the loop would look like.

The Gateway Arch, St Louis, Missouri

This structure was built in memory of the Louisiana Purchase, which was the starting point for Lewis and Clark's expedition in 1804. They ended up on the Oregon coast, completely missing Santa Monica, California. If only they had Google Maps and Alex to guide them like we did. On arrival, we had unknowingly become part of the biggest motorcycle rally in St Louis.

Over 3000 motorcyclists raced around the city (including us – but not the racing bit), in the *'Ride of the Century'*. The purpose was unclear, but it was enjoyable to observe - not so much to take part. A few reckless riders were racing around, and one narrowly avoided causing an accident in front of us. We heard that two people had been killed, but we could not confirm that. We were sure that the police would have made dozens of arrests if they were enforcing the law on these irresponsible riding antics. I enjoy motorcycle rallies, but mass groups like this are ones to skip.

We examined the large arch and snapped some photos before heading back on I-44 to Rolla for a beer and to chat about our day. St Louis, like many large towns and cities on Route 66, had various passageways through and around the urban areas over the years. For sure, our transit today was not on any of those.

This was our first full day heading west. Technically speaking, we were headed southwest, but we identified as the Westbound Crew, making west our direction. We covered 316 miles and spent exactly six hours in the saddle. We had experienced rising temperatures, peaking at 95F - the hottest yet. But it would get hotter. Rising temperatures, varied weather patterns, sightseeing, and riding some of the original Route 66 roads were awesome experiences. Not so much the dodgy motorcycling activity in St Louis.

One ritual we wanted to adopt from this day was to have an immediate beer and celebrate the occasion once we had arrived at our destination. We would all take turns in getting the carryout

Motorcycle Beer, Rolla, Missouri

pack a few miles out from the accommodation. Alex stepped up today and had found some Miller High Life Beer dedicated to Harley-Davidson motorcycles – some things are just meant to be.

DAY 3, MONDAY 2ND SEPTEMBER
DESTINATION TULSA, OK

When Shag bought his overweight monster of a Honda Valkyrie from Bob Smith in Tulsa, Oklahoma, we thought it would be a great idea to swing by Bob's home and thank him for his cooperation in getting the bike sorted and transported to Washington, DC. Both Shag and I had become pally with Bob over the weeks and as we were passing through Tulsa on our way west anyway, we had suggested to Bob that we could stop by, shake his hand, and simply thank him for his help in getting the bike shipped, registered, and insured. Bob wanted to meet everyone, so he invited us to dinner at his house. Well, today would be that day.

I have played and listened to a lot of music over the years and have accumulated quite a song library in my auditory cortex. Even before we retired for the evening, I was already singing Gene Pitney's *'Only 24hours from Tulsa'* in my head. The song is hard to get out of your head once you start singing it. Talking about Tulsa all night makes it even harder to forget. Knowing that we were heading towards Amarillo the following day, it was easy to link up Tony Christie's song *'Is this the way to Amarillo'*, on the back of it. I have always been a fan of the Eagles, and back in the 1980s I used to play their music in a band. Standing on the corner of Winslow, Arizona, and singing *'Take it Easy'* with the Eastbound Crew was something I was looking forward to.

We awoke to another cracking day for riding, and we were well into our daily routine. Kickstands up at 08:30 had been agreed the night before, and we were all on time and rolled out of Rolla as planned. Destination Tulsa (we were less than 24 hours away), with dinner at Bob's house. We had been riding for about 90 minutes, and as is normal when riding, my mind drifts, and I have internal debates with myself on a whole range of topics. We were getting close to Springfield; Missouri and I started thinking about how it's different from other Springfields. The more I thought about it, the more I thought that all the towns looked oh so familiar. Roads with intersections every quarter mile, joined with either a four-way stop or traffic lights to impede your progress. Conductive material is essential for the sensing strips under the road surface to trigger traffic lights. Motorcycles, being smaller, may not activate some traffic lights. However, getting Shag to pull up next to you on his Honda Valkyrie is the equivalent of having an Australian Road Train as a travel buddy. There is so much metal in that machine that the sensing strips are triggered immediately. Most of the road surfaces are concrete slabs or tarmac/blacktop and most of the roads are so wide (compared with the UK) you could build factories on them and still have room for a dual carriageway.

If we had been diehards following Route 66, we would have been weaving through and around towns and it would have taken forever. For expediency, we often just stuck to I-44 in this region, deviating now and again onto the old original Route 66 road. Some of these stretches had broken up and were peppered with potholes, whilst other parts were just unsealed dirt tracks which immediately sharpened the senses as the riding on these surfaces became a little more interesting.

Due west of Springfield, we found a little gem of a gas station called Gay Parita in a small hamlet in the Ash Grove area of Missouri. This gas station had got stuck in time. The owner, Gary Turner, was eager to share stories of the past. Stories he must have told hundreds of times before. Whilst spinning these yarns, he would advocate for local hotels, other places of interest, and local celebrities. As a result, you just had to buy something from his shop - a tee shirt or some other piece of Route 66 paraphernalia (I opted for the tee shirt). The filling station and garage had been established in 1930, around the same time Gary was born.

Gay Parita Garage, Ash Grove, Missouri

Just before we had the group photo taken with Gary, he had drawn up a map of other attractions for us to see on our way through Missouri. However, his map was more like a pirate's treasure island map. The scale was random, and the local attractions (as drawn) needed some interpretation and translation. Undoubtedly, his eyesight had been

Westbound Crew, Surtz, Shag, Sid & Alex, Exploring Gay Parita Garage, Ash Grove, Missouri

better. But it exemplified the spirit of entrepreneurship on Route 66. We were grateful to Gary for keeping the legend of Route 66 alive. Sadly, we learnt Gary passed away a few years later, but his memory lives on.

We tried to follow Gary's local directions, but they directed us down a closed road. The enforced detour took us to another one of Gary's attractions at a Conoco gas station, the Crap Duster. This was some 35 miles away, so hardly local, but fitting when considering the scale on the map. We stopped for a bite to eat, and we sat in the shade and underneath this thing

Westbound Crew, Sid, Shag, Gary Turner (Mr Gay Parita), Nigel Surtz & Alex, Ash Grove, Missouri

that was appropriately named. This contraption was a manifestation of a biplane fitted with tractor wheels, a car engine with a huge two bladed propellor that looked like a gigantic lawn mower blade. A bright yellow plough blade and harvester had been fitted to the tail of the machine. A farmer manikin with a pipe sticking out of its mouth was doing the flying. We did not know why this thing existed or the background to the design. It was just another classic Route 66 *'thing to see'*. Oddly, on climbing back on my bike, I recognised a familiar smell,

Sid & Alex and the Flying Crap Duster, Carthage, Missouri

Entry into Kansas, Galena, Kansas

and on looking down, realised that I had in fact stepped in dog shit. So, our assumption of this contraption being a shit spreader seemed to have some truth.

When you look at a map of the USA, Route 66 should have gone right through Kansas, but it doesn't. Rather, it just bites off the bottom right-hand corner of the state before entering Oklahoma. This was no accident, as we will learn shortly. When I think of Kansas, I think of twisters and Judy Garland as Dorothy in the 1939 film *The Wizard of Oz*. A mere 13.2 miles of Route 66 passes through Kansas. It is still a cool place to travel through and, of course; is another state crossing. Just across the border at Galena, there is a very colourful garage called 'Cars on the Route 66'. This is another time trap that was a tribute to the cartoon film *Cars*.

Several rusty old cars and pickup trucks had been given faces and adorned the garage forecourt. Again, just another example of things to see whilst experiencing the *Mother Road*. Just a little further on, west of Riverton, is the Rainbow Curve Bridge. This bridge was constructed in 1923 and is the only remaining Marsh Arch Bridge on Route 66. The bridge is named after James Barney Marsh, the American engineer who designed it. The curved arch shape stands unsupported. It looked like a very modern design and had aged well, considering it is 90 years old.

Walnut Bladder Shag & Supervisor Surtz, Somehwere in Oklahoma

We exited Kansas not long after we entered it, crossing into Oklahoma from the north, but that was long enough for 'Walnut Bladder Shanks' to relieve himself in yet another state; accompanied by Surtz on this occasion. Shag had marked his territory at just about every stop we had made.

The genesis of Route 66 started in Oklahoma. It was here, back in the twenties, that State, and Federal Highway Officials established the system of numbered routes. It is not surprising that Route 66 traverses across this state and not Kansas. We can thank Mr Cyrus Avery for that minor detour and for officially putting Oklahoma on the map.

Having attained statehood in 1907 and with a past as an Indian territory, Cyrus Avery, a businessman, oilman, and member of the Good Roads Movement, recognized the necessity of showcasing Oklahoma's integration into the United States. Route 66 did just that. Today, Cyrus Avery carries the title of *'Father of Route 66.'*

Not long after we entered Oklahoma, we quickly picked up the Ribbon Road - Sidewalk Highway. In 1922, this road was constructed and stretched 15.46 miles from Miami to Afton, OK. It's the last standing section of nine-foot pavement on the old Route 66 system. It was as rough as nuts to ride on. We really needed knobbly tires for this stretch, but for a road that was 91 years old, I guess it wasn't that bad. It reminded me of my transit through the streets of the Bronx, New York, after picking up the mighty Guzzi from Boston, being in a similar poor condition. It was still cool to ride along this historic single highway, and it was easy to imagine the road being populated by old 'Model T' Ford cars and even horse-drawn carriages. Being a national historic site, it gave us another opportunity for a group photo.

I learnt a little about Oklahoma, or rather its weather pattern, when I was 13 years old. I was one of only two male singers in our school choir. That was before my voice broke two years later. To this day, I still remember singing the title song from the musical *'Oklahoma'*. *"OOOOk-lahoma, where the wind comes sweepin' down the plain, and the wavin' wheat can sure smell sweet, when the wind comes right*

Westbound Crew, Alex, Sid, Nigel, Surtz & Shag, Ribbon Road, Oklahoma

behind the rain…". I think that song will haunt me forever. I didn't know it at the time, but we would experience the *'olde'* Oklahoma weather on our return.

Route 66 boasts many attractions, but one stands out as both unexpected and unlikely in the landlocked state of Oklahoma. That is the Blue Catoosa Whale. A manmade structure designed to entice families to have a break from Route 66 and enjoy a nice cool swim in a small pond. For kids that are not scared to death of this imposing structure, they are welcome to enter the whale's smiley face through its mouth, and then either slide down a chute just behind its mouth or simply jump off its back into the pond. Although

Blue Whale, Catoosa, Oklahoma

landlocked, Catoosa is home to the largest inland seaport, connecting Tulsa to the Mississippi River and the port of New Orleans.

We arrived at our accommodation in Tulsa, having spent seven hours and 38 minutes in the saddle, covering 335 miles. This was also the first day that we had avoided the boring interstates. We caught up with Bob and his lovely wife Debbie at their home for dinner - a little later than we had expected. However, that didn't bother Bob or Deb. We were treated to some real Oklahoma hospitality and a hearty home-cooked meal. Bob showed us around his workshop where he specialises in fixing and refurbishing Honda Valkyries. I must admit, it was genuinely impressive. Bob is an incredible talent; his high-quality workmanship is clear in every single part he touches. Bob's bikes are better than new showroom bikes. Shag did a sterling job finding a Valkyrie that was serviced and guaranteed by Bob.

We also got to meet one of Bob's friends, Russell. Russell was a six-foot-plus, bearded ex-marine who spoke quietly. He weighed around 300 pounds and from the stories he told over dinner, you'd want him on your side in a bar fight. Russell was also a Valkyrie owner, and we would ride with him and Bob tomorrow.

DAY 4, TUESDAY 3RD SEPTEMBER
DESTINATION AMARILLO, TX

Bob and Russell met us at the hotel around 8:00 am and were keen to show us a couple of the local Route 66 sites before they led us out of Tulsa and set us on our way to Amarillo. The first stop was the Meadow Gold milk sign. You can't miss this huge neon sign and structure that was installed as a Route 66 landmark back in the 1930s. We parked our bikes under the structure when we arrived.

Meadow Gold Sign, Tulsa, Oklahoma

Surtz was more impressed by the welding than the sign's historical importance. I thought to myself, Oklahoma should not underestimate the significance of having a boat builder like Surtz endorse their craftmanship. Having examined and discussed the sign, we took a few mandatory photos and, just a few minutes later, arrived at the *'East Meets West'* sculptures.

These impressive bronze pieces of art had only just been unveiled (November 2012). The scene

Westbound Crew, Nigel, Sid, Surtz, Alex, Shag & Russell. Under the Meadow Gold Sign., Tulsa, Oklahoma

depicts a confrontation between a driver of a horse-drawn carriage, and the driver of the new motor car, both trying to co-exist on the narrow roads. These sculptures exhibit an incredible attention to detail. The expressions on the faces of the people and animals are exact. The cross-ply tread on the car tires and the creases on the buttoned leather seats sets this sculpture in a class of its own.

Nigel & Surtz at the East Meets West Sculpture, Tulsa, Oklahoma

Having enjoyed the local tourist spots, we indicated to Bob and Russell that we needed to get going; we were aiming to reach Amarillo before the end of the day. Bob and Russell just said, *"No problem, follow us"*. Well, we were about to regret telling them we were short on time. It is worth reiterating that the Honda Valkyrie is a 700lb, 130MPH, 1500cc, six-cylinder motorcycle. This monster is eight feet long and produces around 100+ horses. It is not a bike for the faint-hearted. It is a very capable and fast cruiser, and neither Bob nor Russell were afraid to unleash their octane horses.

Russell went first, and unleashed his bright yellow Valkyrie so fast that he popped a wheelie, leaving the rest of us almost at a standstill at the traffic lights. Bob on his own Valkyrie, was just as quick and before we knew it, we were off. On the open highway, solid yellow lines were no deterrent for overtaking manoeuvres for Bob and Russell. We all thought that this must be normal roadcraft in Oklahoma. That was until we found out it wasn't. I don't remember who got stopped first by the state trooper, but we all stopped in support. That was apart from Bob and Russell, who continued to ride off into the distance, totally oblivious to our predicament. This was the first time we had been stopped by Highway Patrol, and being a diplomat, I knew discussing licenses and tags would be an interesting conversation. I had experience with this back in Virginia. The further west you travel from DC, the less knowledge and interest people have in American politics and the workings of government.

On this occasion, the State Trooper wanted to examine the passports and driving licenses of the Kiwis. He was intrigued but puzzled by my driver's license, which was identical to a regular American driving license except for the lack of an identifying state. He asked me what state I lived in and where my license had been issued. I explained to him several times that my diplomatic license was issued by the government in Washington, DC, and not from a state, but he didn't understand. I then had to explain to the State Trooper how the US Government works with other countries and how they interact through the US Department of State. We got sidetracked, and my accent seemed to be the center of his attention instead of the reason he pulled us over. After several more minutes of dialogue and light-hearted banter, he was happy with the situation and our stories, and was content to let us all get on our way.

Somewhere on I-44, Heading towards 'Pops' & Oklahoma City, Oklahoma

Even before we had returned to our bikes, he was off like a shot, snaking his rear wheels in the soft dry dirt, generating a temporary cloud of red dust in his wake. The roar of his unmarked, matte black Dodge Challenger squad car, and the ripping sound of the tires was quite impressive. If we didn't know better, it looked as if he was throwing down the gauntlet to race our motorcycles, but we didn't want to put that theory to the test today. Unfortunately, in his enthusiasm to get away, he took off with everyone's passports in his passenger seat. Luckily, he did a U-turn just a short distance up the road and came racing back, not to drop off the passports, but to pass us at speed, almost showing off how fast his car could go. We repaid the compliment of delaying his journey by flagging him down as he approached us, but only to liberate our passports. We all had a laugh, including the State Trooper. I couldn't even imagine anything like this happening in DC. We were in *'Smokey and the Bandit'* country now and it was refreshing.

During our next sprint session with the Valkyrie twins, we visited the Seaba Station Motorcycle Museum and saw a 1979 Triumph Bonneville in its original crate among the old motorcycles on display. Goodness knows how many vintage artefacts exist along Route 66 and in places like this. It must be a treasure trove for collectors. We eventually reached our lunch destination called *'Pops,'* a specialist diner and soda place on the outskirts of Arcadia. This roadside attraction was represented by a 66-foot-tall soda bottle with drinking straw that could be lit up. This modern-day roadside attraction opened in 2007. Almost all the sights and attractions we had experienced so

Pops, Arcadia, Oklahoma

far were oversized. These colossal attractions are impossible to overlook and exude an enchanting allure. You stop because you want to learn about the why? Why was there a bloody huge 66-foot soda bottle right here? Indeed, the 66 is logical - however, many others remained a mystery to us, yet each of these attractions hold a unique tale. We had lunch, debriefed the state trooper episode, and then bid our fellow Valkyrie riders farewell. We were a little behind at this stage so took the Interstate 40 to get into Texas and head towards

Lunch at Pops, Surtz, Nigel, Alex, Shag, Russell & Bob

Amarillo before dark. I couldn't help but point and ask Bob and Russell before we left, *"Is this the way to Amarillo?"*

Alex and I knew we would come back along this route on our way east, so we were not that bothered about missing the sights of Oklahoma City. Just before we entered Texas, we passed through Texola, a tiny little town that would have had its heyday back when the *Mother Road* was in its prime. A town so small that its police department boasts a one room jailhouse. Even Route 66 travellers break the law, just like we did earlier in Oklahoma.

After entering Texas, we then came across two Route 66 attractions almost next to each other in Groom. The first was the Britten *Leaning Tower of Texas*. A water tower that used to service a truck stop and restaurant back in the day. The lean on the water tower was a deliberate and ingenious marketing tactic by Ralph Britten to entice people to visit his watering hole. Once stopped to enquire about the water tower, it was a natural next step to invite people to dine in the restaurant. Our very own walnut bladder Shag desperately felt the need to compare water pipes and yet again, instantly relieved himself. He just couldn't hold on long enough to see the next attraction, which was a mere three miles down the road- with toilets! In fact, we saw this next attraction, miles before we saw the *Leaning Tower of Texas*, a massive 190-foot crucifix called the *Cross of our Lord Jesus Christ*. I got vertigo just looking up at this thing from its base. I immediately thought that we would

Walnut Bladder Shag and the Leaning Tower of Texas

spend more time at this attraction on our way east. This would be a highlight for Padre Paul.

It had become clear that stopping and seeing many attractions would put us behind in our schedule. There is just so much to see and do on the Route 66 adventure. The more we saw, the faster we had to go in between to recover the situation. On this morning, when we were leaving for Amarillo, I had the annoying Tony Christie song stuck in my head all bloody day. I was singing to myself, *'Is this the way to Amarillo? Every night I've been hugging my pillow, dreamin dreams of Amarillo and sweet Marie who waits for me…. Sha la la la la la la la'*!!

The other annoying thing today was my gloves. I lost my favourite riding gloves. I had made an involuntary donation somewhere. Although not the end of the world, little things like this can piss you off for a short while, even when you are on an exciting adventure. I think I left them behind at the first fuel stop when I got distracted, rearranging the contents of my tank bag. I hope they found a good home and were not discarded in the trash.

Cross of our Lord Jesus Christ, Groom, Texas

Saddle time is the part of the day when we are actively riding our motorcycles. Saddle time plus sightseeing, eating, and faffing around time makes up the waking day. An alarm call at 7 am usually concludes at around 12:30 am the following morning. We had covered 394 miles today and spent six hours, 38 minutes, in the saddle. This had been our hottest day yet, peaking at 102F.

Sid had broken away earlier in the day to do his own thing and had missed our riding rehabilitation class with the State Trooper. However, Sid found the hotel in Amarillo well before we arrived and put the beers on ice. That's what mates do. Thanks Sid. We ended the day all back together as the Westbound Crew and celebrated at an old Texan steakhouse. But this wasn't any old Texan steakhouse. This was the Big Texan. There was no seven-foot plastic bull here. This bull was about 10 feet tall and six feet wide and was on a movable trailer! There was no way I could climb on this bugger and ride it like the one in Pontiac.

The Big Texan is famous for its 72oz Steak Dinner, yes, a steak that is 4.5lbs in uncooked weight. If you could eat the steak plus all the dinner accessories like a field of baked potatoes, a bucket of vegetables and a loaf of bread within an hour, the meal was free. If you failed, it would knock you back $72. None of us was that hungry, but we watched a 220 lb man give it his best shot, but it was like watching him eat one of his own limbs. He

Westbound Crew, Shag, Sid, Alex, Nigel & Surtz in the Big Texan, Amarillo, Texas

struggled. The big digital countdown clock above the table showed that after the hour, the meal looked pretty much untouched. He genuinely needed a clock that measured hours and days, not minutes.

Calling the Big Texan a restaurant is not really doing it justice. This place can seat 650 people, has a gift shop, brews its own beer and has its own motel and RV ranch. If we could have climbed on the bull outside, I would have classed it as an adult theme park. When we had finished our moderate sized steaks, the restaurant was kind enough to give us a ride back to the hotel in the Steak House Limo. A sort of taxi come ambulance for those who attempted the 72oz Steak Dinner and were at risk of suffering from cardiac arrest. If the huge bull didn't draw you into the restaurant, then a 27-foot dinosaur wearing cowboy boots with spurs definitely would. This is *'Big Tex Rex'*, a family

Nigel & Taxi Ride Home, Big Texan, Amarillo, Texas

dedication to the Spirit of the *Mother Road* from the restaurant owners. Yet another bizarre Route 66 attraction.

Texas is undoubtedly the largest and most renowned state among the contiguous 48. However, Route 66 runs across the panhandle of the state, which is the shortest route across the state at around 180 miles, less than 8% of the total distance of Route 66. Yet, for me, it hosts one of the most memorable of the Route 66 attractions: *Cadillac Ranch*. I had heard so much about this landmark attraction and would finally get to see it tomorrow, along with passing the halfway mark at Adrian.

DAY 5, WEDNESDAY 4TH SEPTEMBER
DESTINATION SANTA FE, NM

It had become a habit. Every day before we set off from the hotel, we always gave the bikes a once over: oil, tires, brakes, lights, etc. Also, we didn't know if people had been fiddling with the bikes during the night, so we made sure everything was just as we left it. This morning, during our inspections, Alex discovered an oil leak on his rear drive shaft. The usual rag spanner technique would not cut it. Wiped away oil was being replaced from a leaking seal, and there is not a huge amount of oil in the rear shaft, so it needed to get sorted. We didn't know it, but his bike would need some serious surgery. Although events like this are unwanted, they distinguish a ride from an adventure. We had to change our plan, and because we didn't have a concrete itinerary anyway, it was relatively easy. A couple of phone calls later, the revised plan emerged. We were heading to Santa Fe.

If you study Route 66 on a map, Santa Fe is on a bit of a loop between Santa Rosa and Albuquerque. That's because Santa Fe was on the original Route 66. That changed in 1938 when the *Mother Road* took a more direct route to Albuquerque from Santa Rosa.

The decision for us to make Santa Fe our destination was based on two things. First, it had a BMW garage that could service Alex's bike. Next, it would take us northwest toward Bonneville Salt Flats, Utah, for the World of Speed event on Sunday. The downside was that we needed to get to Santa Fe before 5 pm so the mechanic could diagnose the leak and order any parts. Our GPS estimated that the trip was around 300 miles. Easy enough to do in one go, but we had some serious sightseeing to do in between. The good news was that the oil leak was not a total seal failure, so Alex could limp the bike to the BMW hospital.

First stop on leaving Amarillo was *Cadillac Ranch*. The 1974 attraction comprises ten Cadillac cars from 1949 to 1963 vintage, buried nose first and at the same angle as the great Pyramids of Egypt. If you are a Cadillac expert, you can determine the model of the car by the shape and size of its tail fins. Each car is covered in some dazzling and random graffiti. The idea was created by a group of artists called Ant Farm, led by Stanley Marsh 3. In 1997, it was relocated a few miles west from the growing Amarillo city to its present location.

Westbound Crew, Shag, Alex, Nigel, Sid and Surtz, Cadillac Ranch, Amarillo, Texas

We added our own artistic impressions to the display as everyone who seemed to visit the site does. In fact, you feel obliged to draw, write or paint something as a memento of your pilgrimage. What was disappointing was the amount of trash that had been left lying around the cars. Paint cans and aerosols were the predominant items. The trash wasn't noticeable from far away, but the closer you got, the more it distracted from the art and made the place ironically, look like a junkyard.

Next up was the mid-point marker at Adrian. The cafe here is aptly named Midpoint Cafe. I wondered if the cafe had been named by the same person who gave New Zealand's North and South Islands their names. A sign across the road greets you, stating that you have reached a distance of 1139 miles from both Los Angeles and Chicago. The platform behind the sign allows you to pose with a head and shoulders shot to capture the memory of your visit. If the sign is not enough for your photo, there's a thick white line on the road with "MIDPOINT" written in black capital letters repeated three times. Of course, we had our photographs taken at both the sign and on the roads, because we could.

Since Adrian is Sid's real name, there was reason to celebrate by grabbing a bite to eat at the cafe. The slogan at the cafe suggests *"When you are here, You're halfway there."* Before leaving for Glen Rio, we stopped at the cafe gift shop and bought souvenirs like fridge magnets, lapel pins, and keyrings.

Sharing or swapping your motorcycle with your buddies is like sharing your underwear. You just don't do it unless you are desperate. However,

Nigel, Red Dragon & Kiwi, Midpoint Sign, Adrian, Texas

Surtz was keen to ride my Moto Guzzi for a while, just because he wanted to. I had no desire to ride his Road King but agreed to swap till the next stop at Glen Rio. It's always a bit nerve-wracking to ride someone else's motorcycle. I enjoyed it but was pleased to be handing it back and getting back on my trusted Italian stallion. The only similarity between the Harley and the Moto Guzzi is that they both have air cooled V-Twin engines. But even those are different. The Guzzi's 90-degree twin engine has cylinders that double as leg warmers, extending outward. The Harley cylinders just sit there at 45-degrees – they have no other purpose. The Guzzi, then, is unmatched in its dual purpose engine capabilities. From a distance, both bikes look like bloody huge industrial air compressors.

If we thought Texola was a muted town, Glen Rio takes muted to another level. It truly is a ghost town. The place seems abandoned and a bit creepy. There are a few dilapidated buildings and a motel that claims to be the "Last Motel in Texas" (but actually the first when arriving from the west). That this was a bustling town in the 1940s is hard to fathom. This is a place that you visit during the daytime only. I was half expecting us to be met by Norman Bates or Leatherface wielding his chainsaw. We discussed why this place was abandoned and why it's named Glen Rio, even though there's no nearby valley or river.

Crossing the border and entering New Mexico, the Land of Enchantment, was another photo opportunity. The stop allowed us to move our clocks back another hour as we had just entered Mountain Time, the third timeline of the

Alex, Surtz & Nigel, Entering New Mexico, New Mexico

contiguous lower 48. Here, I firmly sensed we had arrived in the western states, a land of cowboys and Native Americans.

Our first stop here was the famous Blue Swallow Motel at Tucumcari, previously known as Six-Shooter Siding. I must admit, I preferred Tucumcari better. This is a true American Indian name. The motel was constructed from excess WWII cabins in the 1940s. It has a striking neon sign and stucco walls adorned with shells. The garages are between the blocks of accommodation, and they display murals from the movie 'Cars', which also included the Blue Swallow Motel. The Hudson car that was featured in the movie as Doc Hudson had been parked in the shade next to the gas pump near the hotel.

Hudson Car, Blue Swallow Motel, Tucumcari, New Mexico

Out of all the roads we've been on, the 104 route from Tucumcari to Santa Fe was the most impressive to date. I could have spent hours riding on one particularly long stretch that meandered up the mountain. I deliberately dropped back on a couple of occasions so I could speed up and throw the Guzzi around these mountain bends. Both me and the bike were loving it! The perfect recipe for releasing endorphins made up from blue skies, warm weather, next to no traffic and a constantly changing landscape. As I was nearing the end of this stretch, Sid had stopped and dismounted ahead of me, and I feared that something had happened to his bike. But it was no big deal. The fairing had become detached and was flapping in the wind. Nevertheless, it reminded me of the vulnerabilities of riding motorcycles long distances away from home. A few tie wraps and strips of tape, and we were back on the road. This was nothing compared to the problem Alex needed to sort on his BMW.

About halfway between Tucumcari and Santa Fe is a little town called Las Vegas, New Mexico. No bright lights, casinos, and massive hotels here. However, it's not a small hamlet either. This town has been home to various groups of people for 200 years, such as native Americans, Spanish, Anglo settlers, and famous people like Doc Holliday, Wyatt Earp, and Butch Cassidy. As we were approaching Vegas, we spotted some well weathered, and dilapidated shacks on the unsealed side of the road. The boundaries of these houses were identified by a flimsy, almost invisible, barbed wire fence.

On display and in front of the houses were several what looked like vintage jalopy racing cars and trucks. Like the houses, these vehicles were in various states of decay, but looking at the tires, they had been used recently. Surtz who loves vintage vehicles and builds unique cars, was extremely interested in inspecting these machines. We had stopped for just a few minutes, no one came out to speak to us or ask us what we were doing. But like Glen Rio, I couldn't imagine us stopping here at nighttime, and looking around like we did. However, it made me smile. These are the random things that you discover on a

Vintage Jalopy Racing Cars, Las Vegas, New Mexico

road trip like this.

We arrived in Santa Fe early and found the BMW garage without delay. Diego, the mechanic, got to work right away and had the rear end of Alex's bike stripped down in short order and got to the root cause of the leak. Knowing the bike would not be fixed today, (no parts) they gave Alex an upgrade and provided him with a 650cc BMW scooter. We all found it funny, even Alex. But we noticed that the guys at the BMW garage understood the importance of helping Alex get back on the road. Knowing that he was away from home and providing him with another set of wheels was awesome. They didn't have to do that. We had only reached out to them that morning and they dropped everything as soon as we arrived to fix Alex's bike.

We found a hotel, checked in, unpacked and reflected on the day's activities. I noticed as we parked up the bikes that the Guzzi had come out in sympathy with the BMW and had leaked Guzzi blood out of the righthand side rocker cover. It wasn't terrible, and I figured I could take care of it until we reached LA. I decided to wait because there aren't many Moto Guzzi dealers in the US. I called it Guzzi blood as the synthetic engine oil is a deep red colour and it looked like the engine was bleeding. The sump of the air cooled Guzzi holds almost eight pints of Guzzi blood, eerily about the same capacity of blood I have in my body.

We hoped that FedEx and UPS would deliver the spares to the BMW garage by 09:30 am, as they had promised. The Beemer was going back into surgery for a couple of hours after getting the spare parts, so we planned for a relaxed start to the day after an early night. We had covered 307 miles today in five hours 21 minutes. This was a higher-than-normal average speed. We put that down to low traffic volume, fast mountain roads, and

Alex loaded up and astride his temporary BMW GS1200 Replacement, Santa Fe, New Mexico

> **DAY 6, THURSDAY 5ᵀᴴ SEPTEMBER**
> **DESTINATION SANTA FE, NM**

Santa Fe is the oldest capital city in the USA, dating back to 1610. Hence, the tourists who visits will find an abundance of things to see and do. But we were not that kind of tourist. We hoped the parts would come in as promised and by lunchtime or just afterwards, we would be on our way. Sadly, that was a bit of a pipe dream. The Beemer garage informed Alex that the parts didn't make the truck. They were now booked onto the pony express and would arrive tomorrow morning.

These kinds of things happen on an adventure like this. Rather than a setback, it's just another issue to navigate. Stressing about it was pointless, so we opted to seize the day and explore what Santa Fe had to offer. Surtz had decided that he should fit a complete sound system to his Harley. He was impressed by the sound systems that other Harleys had been fitted with and wanted something similar for himself. He didn't stop at a sound system and took the opportunity to upgrade his bike with other Harley Davidson accessories as well. I had decided I would try to fix the Guzzi bleeding issue, and Shag wanted to fit some kind of limp wrist throttle support for his overweight Valkyrie. Sid and Surtz completely stripped down the Road King electrics to fit the mobile sound station to the Harley. We conducted all the activities in the hotel carpark. I was the only one who was unsuccessful. A sound system was

Fixing the Guzzi and Modifying the Harley, Nigel Sid & Surtz, Santa Fe, New Mexico

added to the Harley. The Valkyrie could be ridden with a limp wrist, but the Guzzi was still bleeding, albeit a little less than before.

Alex and I knew we were carrying too much shit in our bags. So, we clubbed together and Fed-Ex our surplus stuff back to DC. When you have the likes of Walmart and Target in just about every major town, if you need anything, you can easily get it in these local supermarkets. With that in mind, we were brutal in our downsizing so much that we filled a box that weighed in at 20lbs. I sent so much stuff back I had emptied a complete pannier. By early afternoon, we had completed our tasks and sat down to re-plan the next few days, which is always a little easier (and nicer) over a few beers.

Beer is such a leveller. Beer can make a group of men decide on anything. What was noticeable on this occasion was how much friendships had developed in just a week. The adversity of the BMW oil leak made us all pull together. The team spirit lifted the overall positive experience of the adventure to another level.

If everything went to plan with Alex's bike, we figured that we would have about four to five hours' riding time to the end of the day. That should get us to Durango, Colorado. The following day, we could easily make it to Provo, Utah and then onto Wendover, Nevada for World of Speed at the Bonneville Salt Flats on Sunday. This revised plan would bring us back on track. Indeed, the only hotel accommodation we needed to book well in advance was the night stop in Wendover. We would have no chance booking on the day with the World of Speed event taking place. Unfortunately, by taking this route it meant that we would miss visiting Las Vegas. The real Vegas in Nevada, with all the bright lights, casinos, massive hotels, food joints and amazing shows. To

Waiting for BMW Parts, Surtz, Shag, Alex & Sid, Santa Fe, New Mexico

my surprise, nobody seemed terribly bothered about this aspect. I didn't mind either, as I had the opportunity to visit another time.

The cool part in all of this was everyone agreeing on the plan. As the story goes, Route 66 is an adventure, and everybody's journey is different. This was our journey unfolding. With the new plan in the bag, we finished the day in the hot pool with a beer. We still rode a massive 32 miles in two hours and three minutes. All of which was in city traffic, spent going back and forth to the Beemer garage. We also changed hotels. We were used to sleeping in different beds every night, plus the second hotel was much nicer and it had a hot pool! Fingers crossed for the parts arriving on time in the morning. However, if they don't pitch up, then we will need to develop a Plan B. Most likely over another beer and from the comfort of the hot tub. Tomorrow is another day!

DAY 7, FRIDAY 6TH SEPTEMBER
DESTINATION DURANGO. CO

Whoo hoo! The parts had arrived as promised and Diego the mechanic worked his magic on the drive shaft, completing the job around 1 pm. A successful test drive and paperwork wrap up seen us back on the road around 2 pm, heading northwest towards Durango. Leaving Santa Fe, we realized we had strayed from Route 66's westward direction. Indeed, for the Westbound Crew, the next part of Route 66 would be the conclusion on arrival in Santa Monica.

New Mexico was another state that didn't require riders to wear a helmet, so both Alex and Surtz took full advantage of that whilst they could. Indeed, there

Diego - The Saviour of the World & Alex, BMW Dealership, Santa Fe, New Mexico

would be no need to don their helmets again until we got to Nevada.

Few attractions dotted the road to Colorado. The only tourist stop we made was in Abiquiu, to experience the natural *'Echo Amphitheatre'* in the Carson National Forest. This natural rock formation was quite impressive, and you could hear a cricket fart from a quarter mile away. The natural curvature of the rock formation proved to be highly effective. We made all sorts of strange noises and shouted out all sorts of expletives just to hear them echo. This was a classic case of grown men acting like school children and giggling like them too. Once we had run out of ideas to make noises and shout swear words, we moved on.

Besides the amphitheatre, New Mexico offered little along this road beyond observing the various rock formations, some of which were exceptionally shaped. One looked like a female breast with an erect nipple. Come to think of it, several rock formations would remind me of the female form, but I digress…. although there was not much to see, that didn't mean that the riding was no good. The riding was excellent. Actually, this stretch of road from Santa Fe to Durango, US Route 84, had made our top three stretches of road we had ridden on so far. Traffic was light, roads were in excellent condition, and the temperature made it a comfortable ride.

As we were approaching the Colorado/New Mexico border, we could see the Rockies appearing in the distance. This green and fertile land was a stark contrast to the barren red rock of New Mexico. With the change in terrain came a corresponding change in temperature and a change in the weather. We hit a few showers, and as we climbed in altitude, the temperature dropped from 96F to 77F in just a few miles. I swear I could practically smell and taste the change in the weather. Admittedly, 77F is still warm but such a rapid change is very noticeable on a motorcycle. The rain

Approaching the Colorado Border and the Rockies, Somewhere on US84, New Mexico

showers cooled us down, offering a little light relief from the heat. We stopped at the *'Welcome to Colourful Colorado'* sign where Surtz was showing off his magic photography trick. This involved holding a model car with one hand close to his camera with the sign in the background. The result looks like a full-size car against the sign. We arrived in Durango around 8 pm, having covered some 217miles in four hours and 16 minutes.

Surtz at the Colorado/New Mexico Border, New

DAY 8, SATURDAY 7TH SEPTEMBER
DESTINATION OREM, UT

If anyone reading this is a train enthusiast, then Durango should be on your *'places to visit'* list. Durango and Silverton are connected by a steam train that runs on a narrow-gauge railroad. The journey takes you through some of the best mountains and canyons Colorado offers. This railroad is a throwback from the old mining boom of the 1800s. We got to know all about this railroad just as we were leaving Durango because the train was getting ready to depart. The smell of the smoke, hot lubricating oils and greases, and the sound of hissing steam gave us a taste (literally) of what it would have been like back in the day. For me, there has always been something quite magical about steam trains. Despite not being environmentally friendly, it's still impressive to see this engineering masterpiece in action 140 years later. The only difference was the cargo, swapping precious metals for precious passengers.

Waiting for the train to leave didn't overly delay our departure from Durango. We were roughing it in the local Starbucks, just watching the activities of the day unfold for the local railroad workers. Once we got going, we headed west through the San Juan National Forest towards Utah.

Steam Train in Durango Station, Durango, Colorado

Our destination was Salt Lake City, but mother nature would have a say on that, a little later in the day. The change in scenery and terrain from Colorado to Utah was more impressive than New Mexico to Colorado. You certainly felt at one with nature whilst riding a motorcycle. Repeated blue skies, comfortable temperatures, and very low traffic volumes. The riding was easy and pleasurable, with a few long twisties that suited all bikes and riding styles. In fact, the last thing you wanted to do was go fast. You instinctively wanted to soak up the moment. The natural rock formations were just breathtaking — again. I had so many *'whoa'* moments; I lost count. The breast and the nipple formation appeared again, and that was close to Eddie McStiff's Restaurant

Unusual Rock Formation, Somewhere on US191 near Wilson Arch, Moab, Utah

and Bar in Moab. With my thinking this way, I had absolutely been on the road for too long.

The cinematic scenery Utah provides seems to have been conveniently placed along the side of the road, guiding you to the distant horizon. With the sun beating down on your back, and the warm gentle breeze on your face, you can't help but to soak it up and keep going. My grin widens as I twist open the throttle and I feel the Guzzi lunge forward in sync with the increase in decibels from the Quat-D exhaust. These motorcycling experiences are gold.

Although light traffic is welcome, it was quite nice to pass traffic; it gave you an excuse to drop a gear, speed up, and manoeuvre the bike so that the sides of the tires got to kiss the road as well. The one time I intentionally went fast was when passing a freight train, when the track was running parallel to the main road. These puller trains were dragging over 100 trucks, which made it over a mile long. Though they are governed to around 50 MPH, you must speed up drastically to get past it before the track directs the train off in a different direction. The timing was perfect; we were in a race! These small crazy opportunities become quite memorable in the overall adventure.

We could have stopped a hundred times for photos. There was so much to see. I only had one Go Pro 3 action camera, which was the best model at the time. The Go Pro served as my video and still photo camera of choice. The small handheld Olympus digital camera was really just a backup and for those shots, I didn't have time to use the GoPro. While in Utah, I regretted not having a battery of Go Pro's capturing all the precious moments.

The one place we stopped at was at Wilson Arch, just before Moab and the Arches National Park. The Wilson Arch is named after Joe Wilson, a local pioneer who allegedly had a cabin in Dry Valley. This entrada sandstone formation spans 91 feet and is 46 feet high and has been around longer than the Rolling Stones have been together

Wilson Arch, Moab, Utah

(pun intended). Utah had exceeded my expectations and delivered beyond what I had imagined.

At around 50 miles out from Salt Lake City, we could see that we were heading right into a storm. We pressed on for about another 10 miles before the weather got horrendous. We experienced some insane driving by people who clearly didn't realise that it was pissing down with rain. The roads were waterlogged, and visibility was significantly reduced. There were multiple washouts and specific spots of flooding in the area. Rain is a problem for the Guzzi, or rather the Italian electrics are not compatible with it. With minimal input from me, the lights, indicators, and speedometer all took turns in working correctly.

Everyone agreed to end the day in Orem, Utah. Talking to the locals, we had made the right call to stop when we did. It got ugly on the roads, with many accidents being reported. We took the opportunity of an early stop to use the local washing facilities in the hotel and visit the local Walmart for some wet weather gear. Like the wet weather gear, we sent home from Santa Fe.

The rain had soaked everything I had. The Italian luggage was as effective as the Guzzi electrics in the wet. I emptied my bags, and everything needed to be dried out, including all my electrical charging cords, batteries, camera gear, Red Dragon, and Kiwi bird.

We had made exceptional time, despite the weather, travelling 356 miles in six hours and nine minutes in the saddle. The weather forecast was not much better for the following day. However, if we got out of town early, we would undoubtedly miss the worst of it.

Drying Off at Hotel, Orem, Utah

Route 66 – A Guiding Light

DAY 9, SUNDAY 8TH SEPTEMBER
DESTINATION ELY, NV

Not a great start to the day. We woke to the residual miserable weather from yesterday, made up of rain and mist. Because of the deteriorating weather and demanding riding, we didn't get to see much of Salt Lake City. We eventually put away our new Walmart rain gear and enjoyed some corn dogs at the Delle City gas station, about 30 miles outside Salt lake City

Westbound Crew, Alex, Nigel, Sid, Shag & Surtz, Delle City, Utah

after the skies had cleared and temperatures warmed. Experiencing shitty weather just makes the nice weather even more enjoyable.

Today was the day that we had planned the whole adventure around. And like many travel plans, it was the poor weather that scuppered it. We suspected that the 27th World of Speed event was going to be cancelled because of the torrential rain, and it had. The Bonneville Salt Flats had suddenly turned back into the ancient Bonneville Lake and was likely to remain waterlogged for a few more days. The flats are mainly public land, cared for by the Department of the Interior. They cover an area of over 44,000 acres, but the speedway itself is just 80 feet wide, but a massive ten miles long.

Even though the event was cancelled, we wanted to make the pilgrimage to see where our very own New Zealander, Burt Munro, raced his Indian motorcycle and was the inspiration for the 2005 movie *'The World's Fastest Indian'*. On 26th August 1967, Burt Munro claimed the World Speed Record in the category of streamlined motorcycles under 1,000 cc with an average speed of 184.087 mph.

Interstate 80 is the feeder road from Salt Lake City to Bonneville Salt Flats. Stretches of the road seem to go on forever. The last 35 miles is a dead straight road and its dead flat too! Your speed is inconsequential. It's like riding in a video game where the road continues to unfold in front of you. It is completely mesmerising. When we arrived at Bonneville Salt Flats, it was a lovely day and warm. It would have been perfect for racing. We made the most of our time by buying cheap tee shirts and taking lots of photos, even though there wasn't much happening. The coolest of which was the Westbound Crew and the New Zealand flag set against the Bonneville Salt Flats International Speedway sign.

Westbound Crew, Shag, Nigel, Surtz, Alex & Sid, Bonneville Salt Flats, Utah

A short 12-mile distance separates Wendover, the point where Utah and Nevada meet. Apart from gaining yet another hour as we entered Pacific Time by crossing the border, the stark difference between the two states is on full display. No change in mountains and rock formations here, but the cultural change is obvious. Wendover is a town that sits in both Utah and Nevada – and displays the Ying and Yang of American lifestyles. The main road is divided by a wide white line, marking the border between two states. Utah doesn't allow gambling because it's a religious Mormon state. West Wendover in Nevada, located close to Utah's border, has many casinos and bars that seem to challenge Utah's stance on gambling. It provides a distinct experience. It's as if one state is showing the other state the middle finger.

If we thought Interstate 80 went on forever, that was nothing compared with the road from Wendover to Ely, Route 93. Long stretches of straight road, but with little to look at for about

Riding Along Interstate 80, Heading Towards Wendover, Utah

100 miles. Not boring though. Riding was never boring; it was just an opportunity to reflect on the adventure and on life itself. As the World of Speed had been cancelled, we arrived at the hotel earlier than expected and discovered that Shag had turned 50 on this very day. Therefore, we needed to celebrate his landmark birthday in style.

We walked downtown to discover that Ely was like an anorexic Las Vegas. We had to search for the bright lights and casinos. This was not the Nevada we were expecting. The Silver State didn't disappoint in the end. We found a cool place called the Liberty Club Bar, which was an old prison cell. It got very late, and we had successfully drunk just about everyone out of the pub. Shag was completely hammered

Westbound Crew Celebrating Shag's 50th Birthday, Ely, Nevada

and looked it. His wallet made a rare appearance, so we took advantage of that and celebrated Shag's life a little harder. We had a lot of catching up to do. We had consumed huge quantities of water throughout the evening, but that didn't seem to dilute the effect of the alcohol. Walking back to the accommodation was out of the question, simply because none of us could recall the name of the hotel. Also, Shag's ability to walk was significantly impeded. Holding up the mighty

Shag, 50 Shades of Drunkenness, Ely, Nevada

Valkyrie (and the alcohol) had clearly taken its toll. So, we hired a limo, and our driver carried a local deputy's badge. His moonlighting and showmanship of his badge aside, he safely returned us to the correct hotel, and we were thankful for that. The celebrations continued at the hotel. Then, as we were retiring to our rooms, I noticed Alex fast asleep, still holding onto his last drink - a real warrior! As we would not make Las Vegas, we agreed that our time in Ely would count. Therefore, *'What happens in Ely, stays in Ely'*.

We rode for four hours and 52 minutes, travelling 298 miles. We celebrated Shags' 50th birthday in style and had a limo ride home from an Ely deputy. Tomorrow was going to be a genuine struggle, and we all knew it.

DAY 10, MONDAY 9TH SEPTEMBER
DESTINATION LAKE TAHOE, CA

We were all a little jaded this morning after the celebrations last night. So, no surprises there. Not one of us could remember everything that had happened, just parts of it. We tried to piece it all together collectively, but we couldn't. In the end, we just agreed that it was a bloody good night.

Shag Looking on in Disbelief as Sid Reliefs himself on the Side of Route 50, Miles away from Anywhere, Nevada

What we failed to do yesterday was to scrutinize the road we were about to ride today. We knew it was just one road, Route 50, and that would take us into South Lake Tahoe, so it looked easy enough, and that was the problem. It was too easy.

We were about to travel *The Loneliest Road* in America. Doing this part of the adventure with hangovers seemed fitting. It is called the loneliest road for a reason. Depending on where you start, it could be a hundred miles long. We had minimal traffic to contend with, and the numerous and interminably long

Welcome to Eureka, Eureka, Nevada

straights were repetitive and featureless. It was also hot and blustery with wind gusts that would easily push you off the road if you weren't paying attention, and there were very few towns to stop at.

On the positive side, there was plenty of time to reflect and think about all sorts of stuff whilst trying to shake off a rotten hangover. I measured one straight, and it was 13 miles long without a bend. I did this because I needed something to focus on. It was a brutal morning! Watching others struggle with the monotony was amusing. They stood up and did gentle swerves while doing exercises like waving arms and stretching legs.

There were few stops and even fewer gas stations along this route, but what there was we welcomed, taking the opportunity to either drink, stretch our legs, take a piss, throw up or a combination thereof. The township of Eureka had a signpost that suggested it was the friendliest town on the loneliest road. Truth was, it was the only proper town we went through. We stopped for some greasy food at the local Owl Club bar, hoping that some high-octane food would sharpen up our minds and assist us in trying to remember a little bit more of last night's antics; It didn't! We sat at a large round wooden table in the bar's corner, looking at each other and deciding who looked the worst. There was no clear winner.

Trusted Steeds taking a well earned rest, Owl Club, Eureka, Nevada

After reaching civilization at the end of Route 50, we stopped at a gas station to take a breather and think about the most mentally challenging part of our journey. Again, we concluded nothing other than it continued to be an incredibly challenging day.

The descent into South Lake Tahoe was fantastic, wide twisties with a panoramic view of the lake to the right and the raw forested mountains on the left. Less than half a mile after entering the Golden State, we had reached our hotel. We had travelled some 298 miles in four hours 58 minutes. It was a gruelling day overall, but we achieved one of our highest average speeds. A muted few beers and an early meal saw us retire much earlier than normal. We were all absolutely knackered. Tomorrow would see us reach San Francisco and the Pacific Coast. The end of the Westbound adventure was fast approaching.

Westbound Crew in Reflective Mode, Surtz, Shag, Sid & Alex, Somewhere near California

DAY 11, TUESDAY 10TH SEPTEMBER
DESTINATION MONTEREY, CA

Lake Tahoe is the largest alpine lake in North America, sitting around 6,200 feet in elevation. On discovering this, we wondered if it was the elevation that made us tired last night and not riding the Loneliest Road after our overindulgence in Ely. We were refreshed and eager to see the West Coast today and riding the Pacific Coastal Highway (PCH) - destination Monterey. The feeling of excitement and anticipation was being countered by us knowing that the Westbound adventure was ending. After all, Santa Monica was just a little down the road from Monterey.

Route 66 – A Guiding Light

Impressive Hill Climb out of Lake Tahoe, Lake Tahoe, California

We were well rested, and another beautiful day greeted us, setting the tone for another successful day's riding. Days like this never get boring. I feel I just want to climb aboard and get going, then keep going. The hill climb out of Lake Tahoe on the El Dorado Freeway, Route 50, was impressive. Long sweeping bends and fantastic alpine scenery around every corner. I always find riding uphill to be much more enjoyable than downhill. The engine works harder, and the louder exhaust sound reverberates off the mountains and makes me smile. Combining exhaust sounds with the taste of the alpine forest, fresh air in your lungs, wind in your face, and stunning scenery creates an addictive experience. Even the descent towards Sacramento was impressive. After our initial fuel stop, Sid broke off from the group to purchase some racing pistons for his BMW back home. We would meet up with Sid again in Monterey.

We stopped for lunch in Napa Valley, the Californian equivalent to the Marlborough Region of New Zealand. Although the historic Napa Mill is no Blenheim. Napa has been producing wine since 1872, about 100 years before Marlborough. The trek west towards the Pacific brought us to a place called Ernie's Tin Bar. It was here that we had to decide to turn right or left. A decision we had made dozens of times before, with no drama. Alex's navigation skills had been second to none up to now, but we could have gone either way. However, we wanted to ride a stretch of the Pacific Coastal Highway (PCH), California Route 1, rather than head directly towards San Francisco.

In the few moments we deliberated which way was which, I took a photograph with the GoPro camera. The shot perfectly captured us all. Alex was searching for directions on his phone while the rest of us were doing our own thing, trusting Alex's decision-making. To me, capturing that single moment ranked among some of the iconic shots of the entire adventure. We turned left at Ernie's Tin Bar and went west, which added to our travel distance, but we got to enjoy a long ride on PCH. The weather got bad when we reached the west coast. It was cold, damp, and the roads were slippery.

The way the PCH hogs the coast and meanders around the coves and bays reminded me of the coastal roads in New

Westbound Crew, Nigel, Surtz, Alex & Shag, Ernies Tin Bar, Petaluma, California

Zealand and the Great Ocean Road in Australia. In places, the Pacific was lapping up onto the side of the road, with only a layer of large pebbles stopping it from consuming the highway. Autumn was not quite in full swing, but leaves had fallen and had peppered parts of the roads at the most inappropriate locations. Wet leaves on the newly sealed slippery roads made for some cautious cornering.

The crew had stopped at Stinson Beach to wait for me. I had fallen behind the pack frequently because of my personal quest to sniff out gift shops that sold lapel pins. I had been collecting lapel pins as a keepsake throughout the entire trip and had indicated to the crew that if they spot a gift shop to let me know. This was one of those times. Turns out, lapel pins are not as popular as I thought, and they were getting difficult to source. However, I still spent over $150 on them.

Alex Struggling with his Back, PCH, California

One Route 66 pin from Cool Springs in Arizona cost me $12. That was about three times what I would normally pay – but I had no choice. I had to buy it for my collection.

PCH, like the coastal road in New Zealand, does not sit at sea level all the time. It rises and falls with the geography of the coastline. It was at one of Shag's routine walnut bladder piss

Walnut Bladder Shag marking his territory yet again, PCH, California

stops that Alex first experienced a lower back pain. This would come back with a vengeance during the eastbound adventure, just a few days from home. We picked up the main Route 101 on the run into San Francisco and thoroughly enjoyed the experience of driving over one of the most iconic bridges in the world, the Golden Gate Suspension Bridge. The weather had not improved; it was still cold, damp and windy, but it didn't stop us feeling proud of the fact that we had made it across the entire country with no significant incidents.

Our first glimpse of the bridge saw the top of the twin towers smothered by the low clouds moving through the bay area. It put the bridge into perspective; it was an impressive structure and still looking good some 80 years later. We took two minutes and 18 secs to cover the 1.7mile, six lane, suspended road.

We got stuck in traffic during rush hour in San Francisco. To distract

Westbound Crew Iconic Photo, Alex, Nigel, Shag & Surtz Golden Gate Bridge, San Francisco, California

myself, I thought of Dionne Warwick's song *'Do You Know the Way to San Jose?'* because that's where we were heading. And the answer to the question was, yes, we do! Again, these bloody songs get stuck in your head. But it made a change from reciting lyrics from the Eagles and Gene Pitney songs.

The PCH south of San Fran had road works, bridge repairs and landslide clean ups. I wondered how many of these had resulted from earthquakes and tremors because it's on the Pacific Ring of Fire. This was one of the few days that we had run out of daylight before we had reached our destination in Monterey. Not perfect, but not problematic either. Upon arrival, we navigated to the specified hotel, despite there being a couple with the same name. The probability of getting it right on the first try was 50% and we got it wrong. When we found the correct hotel, we had clocked up 385 miles with eight hours and 41 minutes in the saddle. The west coast's unexpected chill and riding in the darkness made for one of our most tiring days.

DAY 12, WEDNESDAY 11TH SEPTEMBER
DESTINATION OJAI, CA

We met up with Sid again this morning and had the most leisurely of starts of the entire trip. We were leaving from Fisherman's Wharf, Monterey. Coffee, conversation, and some gift shopping were the order of the day, along with listening to a very talented busker. We had all felt that the end of the adventure was just down the road, so we were in no rush to get there. The relaxed mood, having got this far, set the tone for the day. I know we were all having mixed feelings about the end of the Westbound adventure. For S3, they were heading back home to loved ones. For Alex and me, this was just

Surtz & The Busker, Monterey, California

the halfway marker.

The relaxed mood was challenged early on. We headed due south on the Pacific Coastal Highway 1, along with what seemed like half of America. Everyone was on the road today. For the tourist, the coastal road is the only way to head south. The coastline boasts stunning scenery and winding roads perfect for motorcyclists, but progress was frequently halted by road construction and heavy traffic.

Westbound Crew, Surtz, Sid, Nigel, Alex & Shag, Somewhere on PCH, PCH, California

The weather was shitty with wind and fog making the going tough, so it altered the mood a bit. Walnut bladder Shag made use of the ample pit stop opportunities. On reaching Santa Maria, Alex broke off from the rest of us and headed nonstop to Santa Monica to sort his bike for the return journey. The Beemer needed a new rear boot as the one that was fitted had worn itself into a racing slick, plus the bike was due a service. Alex had also planned to spend a few calm days in LA with his girlfriend, Sarah, before trekking back east. The rest of us headed off east, up into the mountains on the Cuyama Highway – CA166.

Truth was, we didn't know where we were heading because our primary navigator and leader had already headed off towards Santa Monica. This was

Westbound Crew & Harley Guest, Surtz, Shawn, Nigel, Shag & Sid, Ventucopa, California

the first time we had been alone without Alex, and we almost ran out of gas after a major planning failure. The only gas station for miles had no gas. It was here that we met our knight in shining armour, Shawn, a Harley rider. Shawn got to know us all and then sorted out some gas for us. He then

Maricopa Highway Road to Ojai, Ventucopa, California

insisted we follow him to a pub in Ventucopa called *'The Place'*. This was in the middle of fucking nowhere! He could have been taking us to our death for all we knew, but that we outnumbered him four to one was working in favour in my own overactive imagination. I think we were all a little hesitant at first, but we went with it. What could go wrong here? After all, he was a biker. Turns out he was a sincere and extremely nice guy. *The Place'* was Shawns' local pub when he lived at home. I don't remember what he did and why he was there, but we were thankful for his help. We had a few sherbets, told a few stories, took some photos, and got directions and instructions about a couple of hotels in Ojai.

Sid, Shawn, Surtz, Overlooking Maricopa Highway into Ojai, Ventucopa, California

Shawn cautioned us about the twisties while driving down Maricopa Highway – CA33 to Ojai, which is a tricky road where we would descend about 3000 feet. As we began our descent, dusk was less than an hour away, leaving us vulnerable to sun strike coming out of the bends. On the positive side, the bright orange sunlight and the evening sky were a beautiful backdrop. The shadows of us riding were being projected onto the side of the mountain and it made me smile. It was such a beautiful evening you just wanted it to go on forever. The descent had a bit of everything: tight bends, long bends, straights, tunnels and, regrettably, debris. The absence of barriers on the roadside was worrying at first, but once you got used to the ride, it was no longer a concern. Debris was more of a danger as it got darker.

I did my usual trick of dropping back behind everyone and then speeding up. The roads reminded me so much of the coastal highway and the Lewis and Arthurs pass on New Zealand's South Island. Shawn gave us sound recommendations on hotels, and we arrived having completed 288 miles, spending six hours and 12 minutes in the saddle.

This would be the penultimate night of the Westbound Crew adventure before reaching Santa Monica tomorrow.

DAY 13, THURSDAY 12TH SEPTEMBER
DESTINATION SANTA MONICA, CA

We had an early start from Ojai, having had a quiet evening. The weather was typical for the West Coast. Sunny, warm and inviting, perfect for riding. We knew the end was in sight, so we just went for it. Sprinting to the finish line was a bittersweet feeling. We had a unique experience for two weeks on our motorcycle trip across America and had become great mates. The memories we made were exceptional. These thoughts had been going through my head all morning as we cruised south down PCH.

While passing Pepperdine University, Malibu, we saw

Surtz & Trusted Steeds, Underneath Santa Monica Pier, Santa Monica, California

the Wave of Flags tribute to 9/11 victims. The 3000 flags in the Alumni Park, which run alongside the road, were hard to ignore. No signage indicated it, but we crossed into the Greater Los Angeles area between Malibu and Santa Monica. This area is the second largest metropolitan area in the USA, with a population of over 18 million. And by the volume of traffic we experienced, most of them were on the road this day.

Those who arrived in the city from the east via Route 66 would have been greeted by the impressive Santa Monica pier entrance and the breathtaking Pacific coastline. But for us, we reached the destination approaching from the north. We had travelled a mere 73 miles in one hour 53 minutes. We parked the bikes under the Santa Monica pier and then walked over the pier for the obligatory photo opportunity at the End of the Trail signpost.

The pier was built in 1908. A sign was erected in 2009, to mark the spiritual end of Route 66. Indeed, Santa Monica is the westernmost point of California, so next stop in a southwest direction would have been New Zealand. In the past, the end of Route 66 was at the intersection of Lincoln and Olympic Boulevard, but now it's recognised as Ocean Avenue (where the road runs out). The signpost was enough for us; we didn't feel the need to identify the end spot. Our signing of the visitor's book at the signpost marked the end of the Westbound Crew's leg, but not the end of the adventure. Alex had arrived on Wednesday night to sort the rear tire on his bike, which meant he was the first person to complete the Westbound leg. This was fitting, as he had done 99% of the navigation. The rest of us shared the remaining one percent and came in second. If we had not met Shawn during our one percent stint, we may have been a day late, and if Shawn had been a serial killer like we thought, we may never have made it at all. Although, to be fair to Sid's navigational capabilities, he had done some solo riding on the

Westbound Crew, Hands on The Mother Road, Santa Monica, Pier, California

trek west and had found the Pacific Ocean without too much trouble.

Although the riding part of the Westbound leg had been completed, we had some serious logistics to sort out. Sid needed to get new tires for the Kawasaki and prepare the bike for Paul to ride the Eastbound return leg. He also had some racing wheel rims to pick up for his vintage BMW race bike back home. These would be company for the pistons he had bought earlier on the trip.

The mighty Guzzi lost a bit of its might in the last few days. The bike had developed a fuel issue and would stall during pulling up at traffic lights and just run rough at odd times. It irritated me more than anything, but I wanted a professional with Guzzi hospital equipment to examine it. The rocker cover leak was never going to fix itself, so that needed to get sorted as well. Luckily, I found a Guzzi dealership on the outskirts of LA and had booked the bike in for surgery on Friday 13th. I am not usually superstitious, but it made me wonder if the bike would come out of surgery restored with all its might. I guess I always had Saturday as a fallback if Friday really did turn out to be a nightmare.

Surtz and Shag had some serious shopping to do and had to find the shippers to load up their bikes for export back to New Zealand. Sarah, Alex's girlfriend, arrived this day and so did Shags' girlfriend, Debbie. So, we all had different things to do for the rest of the day but agreed to meet up for dinner. Sid arranged accommodation near the airport for an easy Sunday departure to New Zealand, and we all stayed there except for Alex and Sarah, who had made other plans.

Standing on the Santa Monica pier next to the Route 66 sign was both a happy and sad occasion. Alex and I were only halfway through, but it signalled the end of the Westbound adventure. The shared experience of riding across the country had taken our individual and

Westbound Crew, Santa Monica Pier, Santa Monica, California

collective friendships to another level. The shared experiences had completely bonded the group. And now me and Alex were about to do it all again with a new Eastbound Crew. Dinner was a fantastic celebration of the Route 66 Westbound Crew adventure and was a very late night. Tomorrow would be a serious *'sort your shit out day'* for everyone.

DAY 14, FRIDAY 13TH SEPTEMBER
DESTINATION LOS ANGELES, CA

Another start to the day with a bloody hangover. Will we ever learn? This was going to be a very busy day for everyone. I had booked an early appointment with the Guzzi dealer, as I didn't know how long the surgery would be. The diagnostics couldn't determine the fuel problem. The mechanic suggested it was shitty fuel or incompatible California additives. He put some super-duper additive in the tank, tweaked the engine management system, and suggested that the issue would disappear completely once we were out of California. The oil leak on the right-hand side was a simple rocker cover gasket. The small leak I had been nursing effectively waterproofed my jeans on the lower right leg. In hindsight, I should have bought a spare gasket for the left-hand side. Although I didn't know it at the time, the Italian engineering would fail me again in just a few more days and challenge my initiative to get a fix.

Surtz at Mainfreight Export Warehouse, Los Angeles, California

Sarah and Alex had hired a large SUV, which was awesome, as they helped to move people to where they needed to be. Surtz and Shag in particular didn't have a ride once they dropped off the Harley and

Valkyrie with Mainfreight, the New Zealand Shipping Company. At the shippers, Surtz and Shag signed the export and ownership papers and then left the bikes to be loaded. We checked the Harley odometer and determined that S3 had travelled 5488 miles during their three-week adventure in the USA, averaging 261 miles per day.

The exporting process seemed quick and simple. The warehouse had many packages, like luxury cars, motorcycles, and boxes of shit that would cost a fortune if bought new in New Zealand. These would all be loaded into the 40ft containers that had been backed up to the half dozen warehouse docking stations. Surtz had bought some flat cylinder heads, and as mentioned earlier, Sid had secured some racing wheel rims to go with his pistons. These would significantly increase their baggage weight and probably raise a few eyebrows on arrival in New Zealand. Surtz recognised the owner of one of the vintage cars. New Zealand's vintage car enthusiasts occupy a small community, so Surtz recognising the owner came as no surprise to anyone.

After we had finished at the shippers, we went for a celebratory lunch at Hermosa Beach, which was just a brief trip from the Mainfreight compound. We finished the afternoon by having a few beers at the 'PoopDeck', a beachfront bar known for its relaxing atmosphere, reggae music, and a place where you can simply people watch. On the way back to the hotel, we drove through the tunnel under the LAX airport and passed a car that had caught on fire. The car was ablaze

Alex, Surtz & Nigel at the Poopdeck, Hermosa Beach, Los Angeles, California

with no fire truck or individuals to be seen! It was scary for a little while as it was pitch black and the tunnel was full of smoke.

Paul and Ian arrived in Los Angeles today and were acclimatising themselves and preparing for the Eastbound adventure in two days' time.

Ian has sourced and picked up his Harley Fat Boy one way rental, whilst Paul worked with Sid on the handover logistics and finances of the Kawasaki.

In the evening, I caught up with my eldest son's girlfriend's parents, Juanita, and Eddie, who lived just down the road in Long Beach. It's pretty cool to catch up with friends on a trip like this and it adds another dimension to the adventure. We all celebrated one last time as a Westbound Crew and held a brief ceremony of thanks and gratitude. Sid had not wasted his time in Los Angeles and had got tee shirts printed for everyone that represented things that were said over the adventure. My tee shirt read, *'You boys can use your dad's ID for a discount anytime'*. This statement acknowledged that I was carrying a US Military ID card as an active-duty military diplomat. In the US, many businesses and organisations immediately give you a discount if you produce such an ID at the point of sale – which, of course, I did for everyone.

Westbound Crew, Last Night Frenzy, Los Angeles, California

Surtz tee shirt read *'I don't care where we go, let's just go faster'*. Recognising Surtz', appetite for speed and his continuous observations that he thought we were going too slow. On the rear of the tee shirt was a list of places S3 had visited during their time in the USA. My tee shirt now hangs in my wardrobe as a continuous memory of the Westbound Crew. Sid gave Alex a signed Harley crankcase cover with stickers from every state along Route 66 as a thank you for his great tour guide skills. He also invited Alex to visit New Zealand anytime as an honorary Kiwi.

Route 66 – A Guiding Light

> **DAY 15, SATURADAY 14TH SEPTEMBER**
> **DESTINATION LOS ANGELES, CA**

This was the big changeover day. A day to unwind before heading home or starting the Eastbound adventure. For Alex and me, it would be both. Sid, Surtz, Alex, and Sarah did some last-minute shopping, then most of us went to check out the eclectic mix of people, street performers, and shops at Venice Beach. We got lucky; a vintage motorcycle rally was happening when we arrived. We finished the day enjoying a few beers and reflecting on the past few weeks. This was a perfect way to relax for a bunch of motorcycle mates. I had fallen behind by three days on the blog site, so I needed to do some serious catch up. I loved running the blog, and I knew the experience would serve me well, especially if I wanted to write a book about the adventure.

Venice Beach Entertainer, Venice Beach, California

The newly formed Eastbound Crew of Alex, Paul, Ian, and myself said our formal goodbyes to the Westbound Crew in the hotel car park. Shag was extending his holiday in the US for a few days with his girlfriend Deb and had already headed off north.

What an amazing experience we had had,

Surtz & Sharky, Venice Beach, California

Eastbound Crew Meets Westbound Crew, Paul, Alex, Nigel, Sid, Surtz & Paul, Los Angeles, California

and for Alex and me, we were only halfway through. Sid and Surtz would head home tomorrow, but not before giving us a Kiwi send off in the morning. Thanks to Sid, Surtz, and Shag for their Kiwi friendship and for making the Westbound leg so enjoyable and memorable for Alex and me. Safe travel home guys.

Right, let's bring on the Eastbound Crew and do it all again….

Chapter 6
Eastbound

We were already on the road and heading west in Chapter 4 before Chapter 5 had begun. Well, this chapter also contains a little more information than just the Eastbound adventure. It also closes off the Westbound leg. By having this introductory paragraph, much like Chapter 5, it allows me to standardise the format of the book and keeps my editor happy.

DAY 16, SUNDAY 15TH SEPTEMBER
DESTINATION NEEDLES, CA

Alex had been staying at a different hotel with Sarah, and we had arranged to meet him at the Santa Monica pier at precisely 07:50 am for some photos at the Route 66 sign. This would officially signal the start of the Eastbound adventure. However, we should have catered some additional time for Paul and Ian to pack their bikes. Alex and I had become good at getting ready, but this was the first time for Paul and Ian, and we had a bit of a faff. Seeing Paul push the massive hotel baggage cart filled with their bags and equipment for the trip

The Initial Loading of the Kawasaki, Paul, Ian, Surtz & Sid, Los Angeles, California

was comical. Sid and Surtz had come out to wish us well, but they could have spent another 30 minutes in bed, because we had some serious loading, reloading and then some, before we were going anywhere.

After just a couple of attempts, Ian had successfully loaded up the Fatboy Harley. We assisted Paul in loading the Kawasaki by using bungees and a few interesting Kiwi weight distribution methods. This resulted in a couple of false starts and a few laughs, as the luggage was not fully secured on the bike. We eventually got it sorted and said our goodbyes to Sid and Surtz and set off to meet Alex at the Santa Monica pier.

Eastbound Crew, Ian, Paul, Nigel & Alex, Santa Monica Pier, California

It occurred to me that Paul and Ian would figure out in a day or so that they had packed too much shit, just like Alex and I had. We promptly took the obligatory pictures at the Route 66 sign and headed off east. The day was stunning, with temperatures hovering in the mid-70s F and a clear, cloudless blue sky. The traffic was a different story. We physically wrestled with the Los Angeles traffic for well over an hour through Beverly Hills, Hollywood, and Pasadena. We didn't stop to do any touristy things, as that would have just impeded our progress even more. Although we were not in a rush, Alex and I knew from the Westbound adventure that we had to cautiously pick our stops. Trying to spot the rich and famous and pick out some Route 66 attractions had fallen off our list of things to do this morning.

The traffic was so bad that we just found the Interstate and got the hell out of Los Angeles. We almost had an accident because of a car driving incident in the heart of the city. It highlighted the risk of riding motorcycles amidst LA's disorderly traffic on a sweltering day. Also, Paul and Ian had little saddle time in the USA, and they were still getting used to riding on the other side of the road. Luckily, we were all on our toes and there was no harm done. That would have been an awful start to the Eastbound adventure.

Eastbound Crew, Paul, Nigel, Alex & Ian Enjoying a Starbucks, Victorville, California

Once we had found the Interstate at San Bernardino, our progress increased substantially. It felt good to be leaving Los Angeles and travelling at normal highway speeds. Alex and I had got itchy feet after just three days in one place. We stopped for our second Starbucks of the day in Victorville to source a phone and sim card for Paul at the AT&T office. Unfortunately, this non-Route 66 attraction took much longer than we had expected. After an hour and a half, we were on our way again with Paul's communications all sorted.

We overlooked the California Route 66 Museum, which is in Victorville. It was not something anyone spoke about, so we simply overshot it. However, all was not lost. While we were at the historic railroad bridge in Barstow, we came across the Route 66 *Mother Road* Museum beside the Western America Railroad Museum. The latter had many train engines, carriages, and railroad machinery outside on display, which looked as if

Eastbound Crew, Barstow Museum, Barstow, California

they had just been parked up on the side of the road and the drivers had nipped in the cafe for a coffee.

The Route 66 *Mother Road* Museum is a small but impressive reminder of Route 66. It's built into one of California's finest surviving examples of a depot-hotel from the early 1900s. There was plenty to get engrossed with, and

Eastbound Crew, Ian, Alex & Paul, Waiting at Level Crossing, Near Ludlow, California

lots of things to spend your money on. The chance to engage with the spirit of Route 66 allowed Paul and Ian to reinforce the purpose of their Eastbound adventure. It had a similar effect on me too, and I was pinching myself and smiling, thinking about how lucky I was to be doing this trip a second time.

We stopped again at Ludlow, an old mining town to rehydrate as the temperature had reached a staggering 115F (46.1C). Not surprising as we were heading towards the Mojave Desert. We also experienced our first and only stop at a railroad crossing. The train was so long that I had plenty of time to dismount and take a decent picture.

Ian on Route 66 near Amboy Crater, Amboy, California

Roy's Motel & Café, Amboy, California

We took a slight deviation off Route 66 to visit the Amboy Crater. This 80,000-year-old natural volcanic landmark is 250 feet high and 1,500 feet in diameter. And to be honest, it fails to impress. There is no real backdrop or foreground to get any context of its size. It looks like a wart on the landscape. The view from the air is probably more impressive. It earned the status of a natural landmark in 1973, despite having existed there for millennia. The road leading from the crater took us past a classic and iconic Route 66 landmark: Roy's Motel and Cafe at Amboy. The neon light signage and the road plainly etched with the Route 66 shield is a timepiece. Whilst we were there, we were back in the 1950s. Established in 1938, this would have been the place to stay in the Mojave Desert back in the day.

At 5:30 pm, the temperature gauge was still indicating 111F, and we were approaching Needles as the sun was setting. The sun going down on the Mojave Desert and the night sky are beautiful and even spiritual if you are that way

Heading towards the Mojave National Preserve and Needles on old Route 66 (National Trails Highway), Needles, California

inclined. Riding through the sultry evening air was akin to sitting in front of your kitchen's fan assisted oven with the door open.

We arrived in Needles in the dark, which was not such a bad thing as Needles is known for being one of the hottest places in the USA. Established as a railroad stop back in 1883, temperatures regularly exceed 100F. Needles sits right on the border of California and Arizona (and almost Nevada). The heat was relentless today, which resulted in regular rehydration stops. Continuous heat drains your physical and mental energy, and hence your concentration.

Heat caused the only casualty of the day, Paul's boot. The heat was just too much, and he lost his sole (soul). The idiom gave everyone a bit of a chuckle considering Paul was a Pastor. Both Paul and Ian were correctly dressed for the slide, and both were wearing cordura jackets, but Paul's was black and so were his trousers. He must have been close to cooking himself in today's heat.

We had covered 306 miles in six hours and 12 minutes in the saddle. A nice long shower in the hotel, a couple of cool beers and a classic large American meal of ribs ended the first day of the Eastbound leg. The relaxed social setting offered the perfect opportunity for Alex and me to get to know Paul and Ian a little better and to bond as the Eastbound Crew. As Sid had got tee shirts made for the Westbound Crew, so did Paul and Ian get Eastbound tee-shirts made for us all. This was an awesome start to the Eastbound Route 66

Alex Enjoying a Good Rib Tickling Laugh, Needles, California

adventure. The first day had given us a bit of everything.

On retiring for the night, Alex and I recognised we had to reset our minds and our expectations, as we had two new members on the team. Paul and Ian were as eager as Alex and I were just two weeks ago. This was their Route 66 adventure, their ride of a lifetime, and they were sharing it with us. It took a few days for Alex and me to get the hang of packing up, loading up, riding, eating, sleeping - repeat. We knew we needed to give Paul and Ian some time to do the same and to acclimate to the USA.

Going back east for Alex and me differed from our Westbound experience. We were undoubtedly going home. It was still a blast, but the group dynamics were different, and our numbers had dwindled to just four. We would of course travel roads during the first half of the Eastbound trip that we never rode going west, due to us diverting up through Colorado and Utah from New Mexico. Once we had travelled these roads, things would become familiar, and we would begin to become a little Route 66'd out. This Eastbound adventure would be neither better nor worse, just different. For anyone reading this and thinking about doing Route 66, you don't need to do it twice, especially back-to-back. However, tomorrow was another day, and I was extremely excited about getting to see the Grand Canyon.

DAY 17, MONDAY 16TH SEPTEMBER
DESTINATION FLAGSTAFF, AZ

During dinner last night, we all agreed on a 08:00 am kick stands up start to the day. Turned out to be 08:30ish as Paul and Ian wrestled with getting their baggage sorted on the bikes. This was day two for them and day 19 for Alex and me, so the delay was completely understandable. Alex and I had our daily starts down to a tee. We had been travelling together and perfecting our morning routine for two weeks, so we had to be lenient with Paul and Ian. It would be a few more days before Paul and Ian had the packing and stacking sorted.

Once we got going, we stopped almost immediately for a photo opportunity as we crossed the border into Arizona. We had travelled less than a mile down the road, but the stop was necessary for Paul and Ian to capture their first change of state on their Eastbound adventure. The dividing state line being the Colorado River. The Route 66 crossing point over the

Colorado river changed several times over the years as bridges have been built and rebuilt. This crossing was not the one we would have made had we approached Needles from the Oatman Highway, County Road 10. We picked up the *Mother Road* again just west of Oatman.

First Change of State for Eastbound Crew, Ian & Paul, Needles, Arizona

If you have ever been to a theme park and have ridden a rollercoaster that was based on a runaway mining train truck, then that may have been based upon Oatman. This town belongs to the time of the Old West. Gold mining started here in the early 1900s and was big in the 1930s. Donkeys roam unrestricted on the main street. You can tell they wander unrestricted by the amount of donkey shit that seems to have peppered the road. We were half expecting cowboys to step out of the bars and engage in a bit of gun slinging. This experience was quite a contrast, considering that Las Vegas was a mere 100 miles to the north. Oatman is so unique that it's difficult to

Nigel & Donkey, Oatman Mainstreet, Oatman, Arizona

believe you're still in the same country.

Alex's back had irritated him again, and he needed to stretch and rest whenever the opportunity presented itself. It continued as a constant source of discomfort for him and would

Cars of the Past, Oatman Highway, Towards Kingman, Arizona

progressively get worse as the days went on. Once we had fully experienced the western ambiance and become acquainted with the donkeys in Oatman, it was time to embark on our journey towards Kingman. The road has double yellow lines and few barriers to prevent you from driving off the hill if you overtake incorrectly. The cracked concrete had been carelessly repaired with poured blacktop, making the road look like it had varicose veins. Small rocks, sand, and dust accumulated on the side of the road, just adding some additional hazards. Corroding chassis of abandoned cars from days gone by, were a reminder that not all cars had a successful Route 66 experience. On reaching the top of the twisties at Sitgreaves Pass, we

Stunning view of Arizona Landscape, Sitgreaves Pass, Arizona

were rewarded with an incredible view of the rawness of the Arizona landscape. The day was stunning, with a blue haze creating a separation between the skyline and the three-dimensional hills that made it seem like a film set. This was western wilderness at its best. The trek down

Cool Springs Station, Cool Spring, Arizona

the other side was equally impressive, and we stopped at a small gas station, come museum, come gift shop called Cool Springs. This Arizona gas station was reminiscent of the iconic Gay Parita in Missouri. This place left a lasting impression on me because of the high price of $12 for a Route 66 lapel pin with Cool Springs embossed on it. I had to have it, even if it meant paying three times more than I usually would. Even to this day, the pin I bought is still the most expensive lapel pin I've ever purchased, but it's also likely one of the rarest. Once again, these remote locations would have been a very welcome sight back in the day. For us today, we were grateful for a brief rest and took the opportunity to rehydrate with some frozen bottled water, which was a first.

Eastbound Crew, Paul, Ian, Alex & Nigel, Enjoying a Break, Williams, Arizona

Paul and Ian had booked a helicopter flight over the Grand Canyon for a late afternoon with Papillon Grand Canyon

Helicopter Tours. We recognised we were running a little late to reach the airport for the arranged flight time. We looked at the distance and decided we could make it if we put our minds to it. The distance was around 170 miles, and the roads would be much better so we could go much faster. The lady at the booking desk suggested we cancel and rebook for tomorrow. She didn't realise what four determined guys on big motorcycles could do. We would prove her wrong.

We completed the first 111 miles in an hour and a half, averaging 74MPH. As a crew we set a record, and I achieved a personal best. I have never travelled that fast for so long on a motorcycle in my life - ever. The Guzzi loved the speed and lived up to its name by guzzling fuel at an enormous rate, rewarding me with a pathetic 30 miles per gallon. This was the most expensive 100 miles we had done. But the benefits outweighed the costs.

Part of the road ran parallel to a train line and once again I could overtake a mile long train. I am not proud of speeding, and with the Italian digital speedo, you never really know how fast you are going anyway, but triple figures were reached several times along the way. We stopped at a little town called Williams for fuel and ice cream before the short 50-mile sprint to the helicopter pad.

View from the Helicopter, The Grand Canyon, Arizona

We had completely missed out on any Route 66 attractions at Kingman, Seligman and Ash Fork on our marathon sprint east. Williams was the last town to be bypassed by the Interstate in 1984, so it effectively had the last stretch of Route 66 and some heritage. But we missed that too! Choosing to enjoy an ice cream instead. Having travelled so fast for so long is exhausting. I was knackered from the constant flow of adrenaline. The 30mph urban speed limit around the airport seemed like a baby crawl in comparison. We arrived at the desk and surprised the clerk, who was close to selling our seats to other tourists.

I had decided to join Paul and Ian on the flight when we spoke to the booking clerk earlier that day. Alex had done this kind of thing before, so choose just to chill out in the airport waiting lounge. The flight over the Grand Canyon was awesome, as you would expect. The canyon is absolutely breathtaking when seen from above, and words can't do it justice. I found the experience quite spiritual too, and that was not because Padre Paul was on board. It was just a feeling I got looking at the wonder that was below me. The Grand Canyon was formed by the Colorado River, side streams, and tectonic plate movement over millions of years. The Jurassic Park-like scene made it easy to envision dinosaurs roaming below.

Ian's Trusted Steed, Harly Fatby, Arizona

After such an amazing experience late in the afternoon, we had to get going to make Flagstaff before dark. We arrived around dusk, which was pretty impressive considering the distance we had travelled and things we had done. Riding through unfamiliar places in the dark is not enjoyable. Being perched at around 7000 feet, Flagstaff is one of the highest elevated cities in the USA. We noticed a marked difference in temperature from the day before, with the mercury dropping to 67F from 111F. Alex was almost hypothermic. We had travelled some 317 miles in five hours and 52 minutes. It had been an impressive couple of days to start the Eastbound Adventure.

Route 66 – A Guiding Light

DAY 18, TUESDAY 17TH SEPTEMBER
DESTINATION ALBUQUERQUE, NM

Paul and Ian did not want a repeat performance of the last two days, and full credit to them. They were on song for the start of day three and ready to roll out of Flagstaff. They had mastered the packing and stacking technique for their luggage, and kickstands were up at the appointed time. However, we only got five minutes down the road, as Paul needed to do a little sole searching. He needed to get his melted sole reattached to his boot at the local cobblers. The rest of us had morning coffee and discussed what the day would look like. I thought that waiting for a cobbler to fix a boot is much less stressful (and a lot cheaper) than waiting for the mechanic to fix your bike like Alex did in Santa Fe. Once Paul had been reconnected to his *soul*, we were off again.

During our morning coffee chat, I was interested in taking a minor diversion about 40 miles down the road to visit the

Paul Sole Searching, Flagstaff, Arizona

'*Meteor Crater.*' Which, as its name suggests, is a meteorite impact crater between Flagstaff and Winslow. The Barringer Crater was formed by the Canyon Diablo Meteorite around 49,000 years ago. It is named after Daniel

Barringer Crater, Nigel, Nr Winslow, Arizona

Barringer, who first suggested that it was caused by a meteorite and not enthusiastic railroad workers who like digging holes. This was a few years before Route 66 came by and effectively made it a roadside attraction. Prior to understanding that it was in fact a meteorite crater, an eminent geologist, GK Gilbert suggested the hole had been made by a steam explosion. A little more credible than the rail worker theory.

The iron asteroid was only about 130 feet in diameter but displaced 175 million tons of rock, forming a crater almost a mile wide and 570 feet deep. Experts propose the crater holds the distinction of being the most well-preserved meteorite crater on the planet. It absolutely looks impressive, but not having seen many meteorite craters, my jury is still out. If it were in Texas, I would have conceded that it was the largest and most superior in the world. Looking at aerial photos, it would have made one hell of a bang when it hit the surface.

On leaving the big hole in the ground, we were advised to *'Take*

Eastbound Crew, Alex, Nigel, Paul & Ian, Winslow, Arizona

it Easy' and fly like an *'Eagle'* towards the corner of Winslow, Arizona. When we arrived, it was *'such a fine sight to see'*. While shopping in the local gift shop, we heard a live version of *'Take it Easy'* by the Eagles. The version was from a 1995 recording in Christchurch, New Zealand, was quite a coincidence. That was a moment to remember, embedded in the Eastbound adventure. A group of Spanish-speaking ladies walking by took some photos of us when they learned of the coincidence. Not sure why, but they were pleased, so who were we to spoil their day? We had become celebrities for a few moments to some strangers. Perhaps they thought we were the Eagles. Who knows? I sang the same bloody song in my head for ages until I realised, we were on the way to Amarillo. Then Tony Christie made another fucking appearance in my head - yes, *'Is this the way to Amarillo?'* Tony Christie and the Eagles have a lot to answer for.

Red Rock Landscape, Somewhere on I-40, Arizona

The Arizona highway has amazing red rock formations that resemble the Australian outback and the surface of Mars. Although I have been to the Australian outback, I haven't physically been to Mars, so I am speculating a bit about that. Another 30 miles down the road, we reached another iconic Route 66 attraction: the Wigwam Motel at Holbrook. What was impressive on the road to Holbrook was the clouds. Once again, it was a warm and beautiful day. The sun hung overhead like a giant heat lamp, scorching the azure sky into a spectrum of different blues, culminating in a pale turquoise at the horizon. The cumulus clouds were randomly scattered across the sky, and it looked as if they were sitting on a glass ceiling, as they all appeared to be at the same height. As they crawled gradually across the ceiling, the sun would make a silver lining on those that were directly underneath. The

Wigwam Motel sitting at ground level created a breathtaking moment of awe-inspiring beauty, like a picture postcard come to life! The motel was yet another time piece with vintage cars and a few trucks parked outside the Wigwams. You genuinely felt you were back in the 1950s.

The second change of state into New Mexico was another photo opportunity. This was very near the Chief Yellow Horse Trading post, where cliff

Eastbound Crew, Paul, Alex & Ian, Wigwam Motel, Holbrook, Arizona

dwellers live in small wigwams up on the rocks. Not sure if that was for show, or if they were real. On Route 66 it doesn't matter, they are all attractions, many of which are there for you to spend your holiday dollars on whatever they are offering. Other than our momentary diversion into, and out of, West Virginia at the start of our adventure, this was the first time that Alex and I had visited the same state twice. The prospect of moving into another state didn't bring about any excitement. It was a case of been here, done that, even though we entered New Mexico from Texas last time.

Eastbound Crew, Paul, Ian, Alex & Nigel, Border of Arizona and New Mexico

Of course, the landscape in New Mexico didn't change suddenly. But it did change as we travelled further east. Although not as barren or harsh as Arizona, the landscape was still dominated by red rock.

Continental Divide, New Mexico

The next natural Route 66 attraction was one I had never even thought about until we had arrived. When you look at a map of the USA, New Mexico is not the state you would think sits in the middle. Nevertheless, this is where the Continental Divide is located. Sitting at 7245 feet, rainfall divides at this point. To the west, it drains into the Pacific Ocean and to the east, into the Atlantic. We didn't stick around for the rain to verify the claim, but the presence of a gift shop on Route 66 seemed to confirm it.

Just before we got to Albuquerque, we had another stop at the Rio Puerco Bridge. Ian and Paul seem to like bridges. This is another one that is in the National Register of historic places. The Parker through Truss

Eastbound Crew, Nigel, Paul & Ian, Rio Puerco Bridge, Albuquerque, New Mexico

Bridge, named after its structure, spans the Rio Puerco. Its construction took place in 1933 to facilitate the flow of Route 66 traffic. The bridge underwent a remodel in 1957 and was subsequently replaced in 1999. Whilst we were there, the bridge looked in pretty good shape for its age. It could have done with a repaint, but then it would not look authentic. I lived in DC for three years and rode my Jetski under many bridges and the Rio Puerco Bridge looked in much better shape retired, than the active ones in DC.

The run into Albuquerque is like finding an oasis in the desert. Our arrival was unforgettable, as the city appeared to rise from the horizon, especially with dusk approaching and the sun behind us. The skyline of blue and red was a significant contrast to the Route 66 neon signs and overhead structure just outside the city. We stopped for another photo opportunity but had to stop anyway because we had not secured accommodation. We had no idea where we were staying.

Alex was not only the navigator but was the hotel booking clerk too. We had got into the habit of seeking accommodation on the day. We did this for several reasons. Firstly, we had no idea where we would be at the end of the day so that gave us flexibility. We had an idea, of course, but nothing was set in concrete. This had worked incredibly well, but

The run into Albuquerque, I40, Albuquerque, New Mexico

it would bite us on the arse in just a few days' time and that would be the fault of one lady called Taylor Swift. Secondly, there are numerous hotel chains scattered throughout the USA, offering an abundance of options. We took our chances since the school holidays had concluded. Securing a couple

Booking Accommodation, Alex, Albuquerque, New Mexico

of rooms was pretty much guaranteed. Thirdly, searching for last-minute deals on some travel apps, being a cheaper option than booking in advance.

We (Alex) had found a pleasant hotel, and the night staff graciously allowed us to park our motorcycles right outside the main entrance. Leaving the motorcycles outside in the car park is always worrisome. You never know who wanders around hotels at night, and motorcycles are easy to steal. So, engaging the night staff at the hotel gives a little reassurance that they will be safe and not tampered with. We had completed 343 miles and spent six hours and four minutes in the saddle. It had been another long day.

We caught up with Alex's friend Dick and Dick's friend Keith for dinner. On an adventure like this, catching up with friends and family who are close by is a big bonus. Indeed, Paul's brother Rex, who lives in California, caught up with Paul in Los Angeles and met with the Eastbound Crew. If your brother comes from New Zealand to visit, it's an enormous opportunity missed if you don't see him when he's less than a hundred miles away.

DAY 19, WEDNESDAY 18TH SEPTEMBER
DESTINATION AMARILLO, TX

Alex and I had our first 'time' mess up in Albuquerque. When we crossed the border from Arizona, we lost an hour as we entered the Mountain Time Zone. So, we were late for kickstands up and kept Paul and Ian waiting. Some karma for them after the first two days of adjustment. We had already lost an hour, so decided to just slow it down today

Eastbound Crew, Alex, Paul, Nigel & Ian, the late start, Albuquerque, New Mexico

instead of rushing to make up the hour. After all, we had no fixed plan. We just sat and had a relaxing chat at Starbucks. Alex used his negotiation skills to help Paul resolve his temporary telecom plan with AT&T. Maintaining contact with his wife and work in New Zealand was crucial for Paul, as he had important matters to attend to. This was time well spent and would give Paul peace of mind.

Arizona follows the same time zone as its neighbouring states, California, and Nevada during the summer, despite being in the Mountain Time Zone. Like Alaska and Hawaii, Arizona does not shift its clocks for daylight saving. And today it caught us out. As we were chatting about the day ahead, Alex and I realised that from now on, we would experience the Route 66 attractions a second time.

What is interesting about Albuquerque is that it has a lot of vintage Route 66 motels and attractions because of its location in the middle of nowhere. The Main Street is well over 15 miles long, so it can accommodate a lot of

Route 66 traffic. For all this, we didn't see much of anything, preferring to head towards Texas and visit the key sites we saw with the Westbound Crew.

Around 40 to 50 miles away from Albuquerque, Paul had begun to encounter issues with the Kawasaki's fuel system and the

Eastbound Crew, Alex, Paul & Nigel, Fixing the Kawasaki Fuel Leak, Cline Corners, New Mexico

engine's rough performance. The bike was dumping as much fuel overboard through the air box as it was using in the engine. We stopped in a car park at Clines Corners, a famous landmark place on Route 66 to diagnose the issue. I thought at the time only Route 66 could claim such an odd yet simple attraction. A gas station, gift shop and RV park just because two state highways, I40 and US Route 285 cross each other.

At times like this, after examining the bike, you are forced to make a decision. Fix the problem completely or try something innovative and live with it, providing it doesn't prevent the bike from being ridden, of course. We concluded that the fuel floats were jamming in one or more carburetors. As the bike had done around a million

Eastbound Crew, Ian, Nigel, Ale & Paul, Blue Swallow Motel, Tucumcari, New Mexico

miles over its 27 years, it was clearly tired and worn out. We decided that a permanent fix would require a strip down of the carbs and we weren't going to do that in the middle of New Mexico.

We beat the carbs with a hammer to reset the floats and clear any blockage. Then we poured in some fuel additive to clean out the jets and anything else in the carb that may be gummed up. Then with some judicious management of the fuel cock, the bike would stop dumping fuel overboard if the hammering and fuel additive didn't work. The combination of the three made life better, but it was a problem that would

Nigel and Lizard Friend in PowWow Restaurant, Tucumcari, New Mexico

need constant attention. The good news was that the faster Paul went, the less of a problem he had. Paul's constant attention to the bike paid off. The bike kept going, so it was game on for Texas.

Next stop was the famous Blue Swallow Motel at Tucumcari. This was the first of the second time around attractions. Visiting the attraction again gave Alex and me more time to see the things we missed the first time, such as the painted wall murals and motel cabins. We were also the consummate tour

Eastbound Crew, Nigel, Ian and Alex, Glen Rio, New Mexico/Texas border

guides and could advise Paul and Ian on the key features that caught our attention the first time around. I confess, revisiting the attraction wasn't as tedious as expected; it remained enjoyable and preferable to being at work. We had lunch at the historic PowWow Restaurant in Tucumcari. For some reason it had a

Paul & Ian, Midpoint, Adrian, Texas

manikin of a giant lizard. The bloody thing frightened the shit out of me when I hugged it for a photo, and it spoke to me, much to the amusement of others. Again, a classic Route 66 restaurant attraction that was full of memorabilia, although I did not know the significance of the bloody lizard – other than the lounge was named after it.

A further 40 miles down the road and we were at Glen Rio, the last or first town in New Mexico, depending on which way you are traveling. I didn't really enjoy our time in the deserted town with the Westbound Crew. The place was still devoid of life, and I felt no safer this time around expecting Leatherface, Jason Voorhees, or Michael Myers to come out and welcome us with chainsaws.

FedEx Truck taking a rest, Somewhere on I40, Texas

Being grateful that we made it to Glen Rio in daylight, we took a few snaps for the album, then got the hell out of there to take

Eastbound Crew, Nigel, Ian & Alex, Cadillac Ranch, Amarillo, Texas

a few photos at the Texas border sign just down the road. Once we were in Texas, it was a mere 20 miles to the halfway marker at Adrian. Reaching the halfway point seemed to come around quickly with the Eastbound Crew. We had only been on the road for four days and we were halfway home. It all seemed to happen too quickly. Although, on reflection, we seemed to cram in a lot of attractions on our trek east, and more than we had done heading west.

From Adrian, we were heading to one of the most memorable Route 66 attractions just on the outskirts of Amarillo: *'Cadillac Ranch'*. However, in this particular area, Interstate 40 is somewhat vulnerable to wind gusts, and we were delayed by two serious truck accidents that occurred close to each other. Having experienced the wind's wrath, seeing a FedEx truck lying down and napping on the side of the road came as no surprise. The wind was brutal, and the gusts were considerably stronger than the prevailing wind. Strong winds on a motorcycle are extremely dangerous. You clearly can't see them, and they can hit you just like someone trying to push

Alex painting 'Kiwi's', Cadillac Ranch, Amarillo, Texas

you over from close quarters. The accidents reminded me of my days commuting on my Suzuki DR650 in Wellington, where I had to lean to stay straight in gusty, windy weather. Wellington was notorious for its wind and good training for Interstate 40. The traffic hold ups impeded our progress, but the wind was relentless and made the riding more tiring than it should have been.

Times like this prompt me to reflect and be grateful that we were not involved in the accidents. With that kind of mindset, I am happy sitting there in a traffic jam, because we are safe. We eventually reached the Cadillac Ranch and made the quarter-mile walk across a dusty brown baron field to see up close the ten half sunken Cadillac cars. Once again, we were blessed with brilliant weather as we headed east on this beautiful day. It might have been the fact that we had a padre on the Eastbound Crew, and he was using his influence with the almighty for our benefit. Alex found some paint and left a lasting image of our visit by painting the word Kiwis on one car.

Alex & Nigel, The Big Texan Restaurant, Amarillo, Texas

We ended the day just as we had on day four of the Westbound adventure, by dining in the Big Texan in Amarillo. The big 72-ounce Texan steak was still on the menu, but it didn't look any more attractive today than it did on day four. However, we did witness a young Asian man give it a go and I am sure he had more steak left at the end of the hour than what he started with. He just seemed to be successful at chopping it up and pushing it around his plate. Highly profitable for the restaurant and entertaining for customers. We all had a good feed. After all, this was Texas. Everything is bigger here, including the restaurant, which was more than just a place to eat. It gave tourists a bit of everything, with a gift shop, gaming machines, its own brewery, and several bars. We had a limo ride to and from the hotel, like we did with the Westbound Crew, so had the full Big Texan experience, once again. The 27-foot green dinosaur sporting cowboy boots remained at the front of the house; a one-of-a-kind spectacle exclusive to Route 66. Another impressive day. We traveled 308 miles, spending four hours and 53 minutes in the saddle.

DAY 20, THURSDAY 19TH SEPTEMBER
DESTINATION TULSA, OK

We had stayed in the same hotel as we did with the Westbound Crew, and things were becoming all too familiar to Alex and me. We imagined what the next week would look like, and although we were enjoying our time with Paul and Ian, revisiting tourist spots again would never be as much fun second time around. This was nothing to do with Paul and Ian. It was just that we had been there, done that. Not only that, but we had done it only a few days ago. Alex and I needed to do something different and allow Paul

The Cross of our Lord Jesus Christ, Groom, Texas

and Ian to have their own mini Route 66 adventure, just like S3 and Alex and I had done before we started the Westbound trek. We would have such a discussion at dinner tonight.

When we set off, we had no intention of breaking any land speed records. But once we got going, we really picked up the

Eastbound Crew at the base of the Cross of our Lord Jesus Christ, Groom, Texas

pace. We rode a 242 miles stint at an average speed of 72 MPH. The last 99 miles would be at an average speed of 76 MPH, beating the Arizona sprint to get to the Grand Canyon tour. I was not sure why we were breaking speed records. It was probably a combination of Paul trying to burn fuel quicker than he was losing it through leakage, our attempts to avoid inclement weather, and our enjoyment of just riding fast. It didn't matter; the riding was still a lot of fun.

If we were in any doubt that we were in Texas, then that doubt would have been completely blown away just 40 miles down the road at Groom.

Everything in Texas is huge, of course, and the first stop of the day was the Groom Cross.

Paul & Ian, Entering Oklahoma, Border of Texas, and Oklahoma

You can see the landmark steel crucifix from about 20 miles away. It is that tall. The Groom Cross, erected in July 1995, is formally named *'The Cross of Our Lord Jesus Christ'* which is exactly the phrase you recite when you stand next to it and look up at its 19 stories from the base. But it represents more than just a Crucifix. The whole site is impressive, full of various religious sculptures depicting biblical stories along with an obligatory gift shop and spotless toilets. We knew we would be there for a while as this was Paul's *'Busman's Holiday'* stop. Paul wanted to see and read every inscription this place offered. He was in his heaven (no pun intended). I thought he was going to wear his camera out as he took so many pictures.

Unfortunately, my everlasting memory from this visit was my laying to rest a massive Richard the III in the impressive and expansive toilets. The previous night at the Big Texan had been busy, and my digestive system had worked overtime throughout the night and had clogged my colon. I needed to shift things rapidly. Turns out, I was not the only one either. I think we all ended up parking pythons at Groom.

The next stop was the Britten leaning water tower of Texas, just down the road. We were only there a few moments to take the mandatory photo that proved we had been there. This was my first sense that our average speed had escalated from the Westbound Crew. We were going at such a high speed we overshot the huge Oklahoma state sign when we reached Texola and had to backtrack for the photo opportunity.

Reflecting Pool, Oklahoma Memorial, Oklahoma City, Oklahoma

The state capital city of Oklahoma is Oklahoma City. I wondered if the person who named Oklahoma City also named the North and South Islands of New Zealand and the Midway Cafe at Adrian. We all agreed that

Route 66 – A Guiding Light

morning that we wanted to visit the Oklahoma Memorial and Museum in the capital city.

The memorial honours the victims, survivors, rescuers, and everyone else who was affected by the bombing on 19th April 1995. It was a stark contrast to the Route 66 attractions we had seen, and like most memorials to be found in the US, was thoughtfully designed (including the materials used), effective, and extremely moving. It never fails to impress me how well the Americans remember tragic events. They never forget. The memorial was meticulously maintained and has different sections, like Reflecting Pool, Field of Empty Chairs, Survivor Wall, Gates of Time, Rescuer's Orchard, Survivor Tree and Children's Area to honour those who died.

The Oklahoma City bombing was a terrible act of homegrown terrorism that killed 168 people, including 19 children. Walking around the site and reading the inscriptions was very emotional. The whole experience forces you to reflect on the event and somehow you are transported back in time, and you can imagine what it must have been like. This memorial made me cry, and it shows how effective and necessary these memorials are. They are a constant reminder for future generations. There is no mention of the bomber himself, and rightly so. He was executed six years after the bombing.

After visiting the memorial, it started raining heavily, so we went to get lunch, hoping the rain would stop, but it didn't. The cafe we ate lunch at offered a special Oklahoma classic of battered brisket! We had eaten some unusual meals over the last few weeks, but this was a new one. It was apparent that it was a *'special'*. I am no cook, but it was nothing special. But it was different.

I don't think Italian bikes like the Griso were designed for long distances or adverse weather. When we finally left, it was still raining, and the weather didn't really improve. The Italian electrics of the Guzzi couldn't resist water in heavy rain, and it showed weaknesses about two miles out of the city. The digital speedometer on the Guzzi is fed by a sensor on the rear wheel, which when wet, seems to turn into a random number generator feeding the speedo with numbers ranging from zero to 156 MPH, whilst sitting at a red traffic light. On moving off, it could go from a stationary 5 MPH to a staggering 70 MPH in first gear, and in less than a second. If only! This continued with some variation for about four miles and was a constant distraction for me. Distractions are not what you want when it's pouring down with rain. To make matters worse, the fricking headlight bulb blew immediately afterwards, probably out of sympathy with the speedo sensor. The speedo had done something similar before, showing that this was an annoyingly intermittent problem that just seemed to be more prominent in the wet. The issue would then mysteriously disappear before I could diagnose exactly where the fault was. Despite its humour and entertainment value, it was incredibly frustrating.

Alex & Nigel and Father/Son Bikers, Pops Diner, Arcadia, Oklahoma

Because of our weather delay, we were late arriving at 'Pops', Arcadia, to show Paul and Ian the 66-foot-tall soda bottle. In the car park, as we were leaving, we got chatting to a father and son who were eyeing over our bikes. Despite his age and difficulty walking – even with a walking stick, the dad felt like a teenager again on his Can-Am three-wheeler. His fifty something year old son, who was riding his own motorcycle, said that his dad would never give up riding.

Eastbound Crew, Ian, Paul & Nigel, East Meets West Attraction, Tulsa, Oklahoma

That made me smile and made me think that one day, I will be that same man. Conversing in the car park caused us a further delay, resulting in the Seba Motorcycle Museum being closed by the time we had arrived.

All these delays made our arrival in Tulsa so late that it was dark. The good news was that the '*East Meets West*' Route 66 attraction was floodlit, which seem to make the bronze statues come to life. The Meadow Gold neon sign was also lit up, and that, too, seemed more impressive in the dark. It seemed like fate. Arriving in the dark is not ideal. But in this case, it was perfect. Our prior experience travelling west allowed us to navigate confidently in the dark without concern for our destination. Arriving at our accommodation in Tulsa, we had clocked up 378 miles (which included four additional miles for the broken Speedo) and had spent six hours 42 minutes in the saddle. It had been a long day. Although it had not been the best day weather wise, that is the nature of adventures; some days are going to be better than others – no two days are ever the same. However, when you are doing

Meadow Gold Attraction at Night, Tulsa, Oklahoma

something that you love to do every day, then life is pretty good, and the weather is just another variable.

Whilst at dinner at the local Irish Pub, we discussed the events of the day and what the journey from here on in would look like. The trip east had given Alex and me too many déjà vu moments, and although we were happy to continue into Chicago with Paul and Ian, there was a perfect opportunity for

Alex and I to do something a little different. We suggested that Alex and I could continue east while Paul and Ian head northeast towards Chicago on their own mini Route 66 adventure. This plan would also mean that Alex and I would get back home a little earlier, although that was never an aim, just a fact.

I had mixed feelings about this plan as Paul was a close friend of mine and I wanted to spend more time with him. All four of us were getting along just fine. However, the idea of covering the same ground as the Westbound Crew for the last five days of the adventure wasn't appealing after 22 days on the road. Consensus was reached. We would break into two groups the following day and do two separate mini adventures. Much like S3 had done before. Paul intended to ride back to Washington, DC, from Chicago (but solo). Paul would then stay with me for a few days so we could hang out together and then he would leave the Kawasaki behind for me to sell. Ian would fly back to New Zealand from Chicago after dropping off his Fat Boy Harley one-way rental.

Alex and I planned to head east, explore new roads, go to Nashville, and ride Route 129 along the *'Tail of the Dragon'* to Deals Gap. The weather was looking awful tomorrow, so things could change. We would remain flexible with our plans.

DAY 21, FRIDAY 20TH SEPTEMBER
DESTINATION MOUNTAIN HOME, AR

Alex and I checked the weather the night before. Since it looked bad in the morning, we planned to start in the early afternoon. We would chase the weather instead of trying to beat it and spend the day staying ahead of it. I felt a little sad that Paul and Ian were breaking off and heading towards Chicago, but knew it was the right thing to do. Paul and Ian's joint trip from New Zealand presented a wonderful opportunity to create shared memories to discuss upon their return. Alex and I used the late start to plan the rest of our adventure. We had already decided that we were going to visit Nashville, Tennessee.

Paul and Ian set off a little earlier and had made it as far as Afton after visiting a car museum just 78 miles up the road. At that rate, they would take over a week to get to Chicago. But this was their adventure. They could go as

Route 66 – A Guiding Light

Entering Arkansas from Oklahoma, Siloam Springs, Arkansas

fast or as slow as they wanted. However, Ian had not been feeling well and hadn't felt great since the start, so a short day would have suited them perfectly.

Alex and I did much better making it to Mountain Home, Arkansas, three times the distance. I realized that our departure towards the east from Tulsa meant we would no longer encounter any Route 66 attractions. From here on in, this would be another sub-adventure. Route 66 had been our guiding light.

Technically, Alex and I could have jumped off the trail at any point once we had hit Santa Rosa in New Mexico with the Eastbound Crew and declared we had ridden Route 66. The fact that we broke away in Tulsa having shared for a second time the '*East Meets West*' attraction with both crews, was a serendipitous moment. Alex and I would now cross state lines we had not crossed before.

Indeed, this would be the first time I had ridden through Arkansas and Tennessee.

While planning our next sub-adventure in the Hotel Cafe over our morning coffee, a stranger suggested we attend a motorcycle rally in Fayetteville on our way to Mountain Home. With no other plan other than

Motorcycle Rally, Fayetteville, Arkansas

avoiding the weather, we took his advice and called in to the motorcycle rally. I am so glad we did; it was awesome. It was so good; I bought the tee shirt!

The event was called 'Bikes, Blues and BBQ's'. The township was completely taken over by thousands

Nigel & New Tee Shirt, Fayetteville, Arkansas

of bikers, creating an authentic party atmosphere. Bikes of various types were scattered throughout the town and were parked in just about every bit of available space. The scarcity of BMWs was matched only by the singularity of my Moto Guzzi. Everyone seemed to be enjoying themselves - even the local police were taking part! There were market stalls, food trucks, alcohol, and other drinking stations and a smorgasbord of local business stalls. This

was more than just a motorcycle rally, it was a whole community event. We stayed long enough for the bad weather to move further east and away from us.

This, once again, was yet another occasion that made me reflect on the positive and unexpected things

Dusk, Mountain Home, Arkansas

that can happen on an adventure like this. Every day is different, and we would never have heard about the rally had it not been for this random chap who clearly identified us as bikers at the hotel. Talking to locals and getting local knowledge is priceless. Just speaking to people anywhere whilst travelling is such a great experience. You never know what you will learn or what will come of it.

We were notified through social media channels that Shag and his girlfriend Deb, had gotten engaged. Shags proposal of Marriage to Debbie got the thumbs up! I reported on the blog: *Sep. 20, 2013. The Route 66 Blog site is pleased to announce the engagement of Debbie Lamb to Shag (Brett) Shanks. Shag took the opportunity to propose whilst here in the USA after doing Route 66. They will join names and become the classic Lamb-Shanks! All the best to you both from the Westbound and Eastbound Teams: Nige, Alex, Sid, Surtz, Paul, and Ian.*

Alex and I arrived in Mountain Home at dusk, dry but tired. We were welcomed by a beautiful blended red, blue, and purple cirrocumulus clouded night sky. A fantastic way to close the day off. We had travelled 243 miles and had spent four hours and 57 minutes in the saddle. We were well behind the weather front that had clearly passed through all the towns we had travelled through. Although motorcycles can't speak, I knew the Guzzi was grateful for me not subjecting it to more rain. The speedo had been working fine all day. Nevertheless, the Guzzi had one other little surprise for me. Although Italians excel at crafting visually appealing motorcycles, their prowess in engineering is not guaranteed to be of the same calibre.

DAY 22, SATURDAY 21ST SEPTEMBER
DESTINATION NASHVILLE, TN

Expectations for today were high. We were going to Nashville. I had never been there before, and I was really excited about it. As a former member of a rock and pub band in the UK during the 1980s, several country songs we performed had roots in Nashville, making it a significant location for me beyond just being a city. It was the music mecca of the world, and I was looking forward to having the total Nashville music scene experience. But be careful what you wish for. The welcome to paradise sign on one of the club billboards just read: '*Eat, Drink Rock*'. I would skilfully do two out of the three and live to regret that I never really got to do the first one.

Stretch of Road Somewhere on M0142, Missouri

On leaving Mountain Home, we headed northeast towards Missouri. This would be the second time on the trip we had entered this state, and on crossing the state line, we immediately picked up route MO142. This road turned out to be one of the best motorcycling roads we had ridden on all trip, but it would come at a cost. The weather was perfect: dry, clear skies, and great riding temperatures. For 42 miles, this was a biker's heaven: smooth high camber lanes, undulating hills, loads of high-speed twisties, very low traffic volume and some great scenery if you had the inclination to look. Alex and I were smiling like Cheshire cats at the end.

The smile instantly changed to despair when I looked down to see what was causing the higher-than-normal heat on my left leg. The mighty Italian stallion had once again shit itself and had blown the left-

Alex & Nigel, Entering Missouri from Arkansas, Mammoth Spring, Arkansas

Welcome to Nashville Sign, Nashville, Tennessee

hand rocker cover gasket and was dumping hot, dark red, engine oil (Guzzi blood) all over my trousers, the engine, and the left-hand exhaust. At speed, the airflow had atomised the hot oil, and it had sprayed everywhere with my jeans soaking up the majority. The heat of the left-hand exhaust header pipe was smoking nicely as it slowly burnt off residual oil. Having ridden many two stroke motorcycles, the smell of burning engine oil is a very different smell to the oil mixed in a two-stroke engine.

My heart sunk. '*Fuck*', here we go again! My jeans were now entirely ruined, but waterproofed. The two-tone denim and oil stain colouring looked kind of stylish in a traditional motorcycle apparel sort of way. But this was the least of my troubles. The bike now had an open wound and was losing a lot of Guzzi blood. I needed to find and apply a tourniquet and get the Guzzi into surgery ASAP. This was the same fault that happened on the right-hand rocker cover going west. Except this time,

Nigel on Broadway, Nashville, Tennessee

it was much, much worse.

I had been carrying a small hotel towel in my bag that I used to clean my visor of all the kamikaze insects that had attempted to crash into my face during the day. The towel was wrapped into a ball, and I held it in place on the cylinder head by pressing down with my knee. I had limited success, but we limped through Missouri into Kentucky and then into Tennessee. At every intersection and stop sign, I wiped the leaking oil from the cylinder head to avoid it dripping on the exhaust. Others would have found it very odd to see a motorcycle with a towel around half the engine and blue smoke coming from the front and not the back. Slight adjustments of the tourniquet whilst in motion were necessary to prevent the oil either burning my leg or causing a flash fire on the exhaust.

When we reached the Cairo crossing, where the Mississippi and Ohio rivers meet, we had entered Illinois without realising it. This was the second time we had done four states in a day. Alex and I knocked out four states in a day on our way to the start of the Westbound adventure in chapter four. That day we had travelled through Pennsylvania, Virginia, Maryland, and West Virginia.

We got to Nashville in the early evening and planned to fix the oil leak on Sunday morning. We had travelled some 389 miles and had spent seven hours 36 minutes in the saddle. It had been a lengthy day, and the stage was set for it to be a lengthy night.

We had no trouble finding a place to stay the entire trip, so we thought it would be easy in Nashville on a Saturday night. Checking for a live concert in town never crossed our minds. Not only was there a concert, but the artist was none

Great Entertainment, Layla's Bar, Nashville, Tennessee

Acrobatic Piano Player, Layla's Bar, Nashville, Tennessee

other than Taylor Swift. As a result, Nashville was chock-a-block full. Nothing seemed available.

Both Alex and I spent almost an hour pacing the sidewalk whilst ringing around all the hotels we could find on google maps. Each hotel quoted rates that had gone through the roof, and then followed it up by telling us there were no rooms available anyway. Alex eventually had success with the 18th hotel. We ended up staying quite close to Broadway, which was great, very close to the bars and music. We secured the only room they had, and it wasn't a guest room at all. It was a cramped attic space with a solo bed and convertible sofa that smelled like an old people's home. This Alice in Wonderland room seemed to be made up from pieces of leftover furniture from remodelled homes over the last four decades. We had no choice, our only other option at this stage was to sleep on the street. We forked out three times the usual fee for the privilege. But it was worth it.

Once we got settled into the attic closet, we headed off downtown to enjoy everything Nashville offered us. I was like a kid in a theme park. So many bars, so much music and so much to DRINK! I needed to put the troubles of the Guzzi to one side just for tonight and let my hair down. Unfortunately, I let it down so far; I was tripping over it. You would have thought that a 53-year-old man would know better than to go out drinking, having nothing to eat first. Nope! I was concerned about my bike; I was tired, and I just wanted to focus on the bars, music, and the general party atmosphere. I forgot to eat because we were having too much fun drinking, singing and moving from bar to bar with crowds of other people, not all of whom had tickets for Taylor Swift. Parts of the night became a bit of a blur whilst other parts I don't remember at all! Although, whilst staggering back to the attic room at the hotel, I remember Alex getting obsessed with a noisy tree that had been occupied by birds or cicadas or something. To settle his curiosity, he simply started to shake the shit out of the tree, hoping that whatever was making the noise would reveal itself. We know that beer clouds judgement, but it also

Live Music, Broadway, Nashville, Tennessee

makes events like that extremely funny. Clearly, we were both worse for wear, but we needed to let off some steam. No regrets. That feeling would come in the morning. Luckily, Alex was still a little more sensible than me at this juncture and got both of us back to the hotel safely.

The entertainment everywhere was phenomenal. I noticed that many of the musicians moved around the bars, playing with other musicians. Each band functioned like a football club, substituting players depending on the gig's progress. It was quite a unique experience. Of all the bands we saw that night, the one memorable band was playing at Layla's Honkey Tonk Bar on Broadway. No idea what they called themselves, but they were entertainers 100%.

The larger-than-life bass player had the classic bass player's face looking like someone who is busting for a piss and standing in a long queue for the restroom. Other than moving his fingers on the fretboard, he sat motionless on the bar stool. The drummer's arm movements were so fluid and wild, he reminded me of Animal from The Muppets. The long-haired guitarist appeared to be Cousin IT from the Addams Family and spent his time shaking his head while staring at the floor. The pianist and lead singer was a talented gymnast who could play the piano in unconventional ways, such as upside down and with his hands and feet simultaneously. He also played a mean mouth organ. Brilliant! Everyone was dancing everywhere and just having a fabulous time generating a fantastic atmosphere.

We had one of the best nights we had had anywhere so far. If you ever visit Tennessee, a night out in Nashville is a must. Just check that Taylor Swift isn't in town. Paul and Ian successfully made it to Pacific, Missouri on their trek up Route 66 to Chicago.

> # DAY 23, SUNDAY 22ND SEPTEMBER
> # DESTINATION CROSSVILLE, TN

Sunday arrived much sooner than I would have liked. I was feeling like crap, had a stinking hangover and now I had to fix a giant oil leak on the Guzzi. Alex looked better than I did, but he, too, was feeling a little under the weather. We both agreed that we had a great night in the bars, and my introductory first night in Nashville did not disappoint. Even though we never saw Taylor Swift or got invited to her afterparty gig. As they say, *'what happens in Nashville stays in Nashville'*. That's because we couldn't remember much of what happened, anyway. We wanted to start the day quietly, so we meandered downtown to see the place in daylight, trying to remember what happened the night before. We failed. We were surprised to find out that there are a ton of bars in Nashville, and last night we only managed to check out a few of them. We both agreed to come back and give it another shot sometime in the future.

I reflected a little on the issues we had faced on this adventure and how many were Guzzi related. Despite having only two cylinders, each of them had failed separately. The first oil leak appeared in New Mexico, and the second one going through Missouri. I had a fuel issue in California, and a blown headlight and spurious speedo in Oklahoma, and we were still a few days from home. What would be next? It made me chuckle too, because these events, as unwanted as they are, made the adventure real and were still much better than being at work. A fact I had to keep reminding myself.

Fixing the oil leak on the Guzzi was the priority, and I was doing this under challenging circumstances. I still had a thumping hangover. I had bought some sealant gunk from an auto store prior to arriving in Nashville to prepare for today's attempt. The idea was quick and simple. Seal the leak from the outside by slapping the whole tin of this brown, shitty, gooey stuff that would go hard with heat over the top of the engine. Once set, it would have sealed the hull of the Titanic. But everyone knows what happened to the

Titanic. Once applied, the left-hand cylinder resembled the aftermath of a bike's tumble into a pile of cow shit. It was pretty ugly, but it worked, and I didn't care what it looked like, it was only temporary until we got home. Unfortunately, the sealant worked for precisely 12 miles. No mention of that on the tin.

As we were leaving Nashville, a brown blister formed on the cylinder head, bulging with Guzzi blood. The thing eventually burst, causing a major haemorrhage. We could travel no further. Even the bigger hotel towel I had acquired was

Nigel Fixing the Guzzi in a Parking Lot, Just Outside Nashville, Tennessee

not enough to contain it. It demanded repair, and it was Sunday! Yesterday, when I called the only Guzzi shop in Tennessee, they had no spares. Even if they did, they would be closed on Sunday, anyway. A short reflective moment and some Kiwi ingenuity got me thinking.

When I was a teenager, I got a moped engine running by making gaskets out of a cereal box. They didn't last long, but they worked. I could do the same here. We found a car AutoZone store that had a sheet of gasket making material. I removed the rocker cover but had one hell of a job trying to get the brown sealant off. That stuff definitely worked on areas that weren't leaking. Once I had cleaned the mating surface of the rocker cover, I applied a smear of oil around the base of the cover to make an imprint onto the gasket material. I meticulously cut it out using a pair of child paper scissors I purchased from CVS (the pharmacy) and punched the screw holes in the gasket with a paper hole punch, also bought from CVS. Turns out that the paper hole punch was the exact same diameter as the rocker head screws. I did all this on the workshop floor of the parking lot. Two hours later, I restarted the engine, and the oil leak was cured. A high five, a celebratory coffee and a savoury pastry in Starbucks concluded the fix. My head had started to feel a little better, too. The fix was permanent and would last until the next service was due.

When the Guzzi is playing up or has broken down, I often refer to it as the *'Gutzi'* and not a Guzzi or Griso, its proper name. Apart from the American pronunciation, which is very similar (Guzzi = Gutzi), the name Gutzi reflects both the way I feel about the bike at that time, and how the bike has been built. Normally, I am a little stressed and concerned about the bike, a similar feeling when a loved one is not well, and you are concerned about their health. The Moto Guzzi is built like an agricultural tractor – albeit a nice looking one. This 500lb naked café racer/sports bike is fitted with a robust, uncomplicated engine and sealed transmission. Even a mechanic with basic skills could diagnose and fix most of the faults with the onboard tool kit and some other basic tools like a pair of scissors and a hole punch! Nothing ever fails so badly that the bike is unrideable. The bike then has guts! And if something (or someone) is gutsy, they have spirit, courage, and determination. So, although the bike has presented me with a few issues that concern me, I know I can still ride it, even after open heart surgery on the engine in a parking lot.

The day was wasted in terms of riding distance, so we decided we would make it to Crossville. That would put us to within 100 miles of the motorcycle resort of Deals Gap. Tomorrow, we would ride the *'Tail of the Dragon'*.

I had read a glossy pamphlet

Another Arrival in the Dark, Alex Unpacking, Crossville, Tennessee

about this road called *'Tail of the Dragon'*. A twisty road that had 318 turns in an 11-mile stretch and would take us from Tennessee into North Carolina. I was determined not to ride on this road with a hangover.

We got to Crossville later than expected, having ridden 119 miles and spending just two hours and 50 minutes in the saddle. A little more than the time I had spent sitting on the floor in the car park fixing the Gutzi. A quiet night was necessary if we were going to slay the dragon tomorrow, and we were both in serious need of sleep. We had a couple of beers and ordered a pizza from the internet. The other half of the Eastbound Crew, Paul and Ian had successfully made it to Springfield, Illinois. They were just 200 miles from the Chicago start point and would end the Eastbound adventure tomorrow. We didn't know it at the time, but we would also end our adventure tomorrow. Monday 23rd September would be our last and longest day of the entire trip and would end in a most unusual manner.

DAY 24, MONDAY 23RD SEPTEMBER
DESTINATION ARLINGTON (HOME), VA

We knew we needed an early start as we would lose another hour soon after we headed further east in Tennessee bringing us back on Eastern Standard Time from Central Time. We were up at 6:00am and were on the road for 7:00am. This was the earliest yet. Indeed, this last day would be the day of many firsts. Earliest start, coldest start, longest day, most miles, injury, truck ride, midnight crossing. We just didn't know all this yet.

We were keen to ride the Tail of the Dragon at Deals Gap by midday and we were just over 100 miles away. The ride out of Crossville was chilly and a little misty. Alex even donned his coat; it was that cold. You could see your

Dressing for the Cold and the Dragon, Alex, Crossville, Tennessee

own breath and feel the dense air saturate your lungs, enriching your blood and waking up your whole body. It felt good to be awake without a hangover and I sensed that my energy levels had fully recuperated. Our alertness was tested pretty early

House on the Move, Somewhere on Route 129, Near Chilhowee, Tennessee

on when a huge truck carrying a house appeared between the tree line as we approached a left-hand bend. Luckily, the truck had a lead vehicle, otherwise we would have been forced off the road. We were forced to stop anyway, as the width of the house consumed more than two-thirds of the whole road. I took this event as a warning that these single carriageway double yellow lined roads were unpredictable to oncoming traffic.

The low-lying mist in the valley looked a little eerie. The cirrocumulus clouds had fallen from the sky overnight and were just hovering above the middle of the Chilhowee Lake like smoke on the water. The clouds faded slightly as they approached the banks of the lake and Route 129. It seemed an appropriate setting to be riding such a challenging and dangerous stretch of road. My imagination

Deals Gap Resort, Nigel at the Dragon, Deals Gap, North Carolina

was working overtime. I felt as if I was entering the Dragons' Lair.

The '*Tail of the Dragon*' is extremely popular for bikers and the local police know it. Although, to be fair, it probably does need to be closely monitored as the road is a Mecca for all sorts of motorcyclists which makes it a potential death trap, particularly if two riders misjudge the same corner but are travelling in opposite directions. The road itself is in great condition, and has several lay-bys so you can stop, rest and watch the traffic. A few were populated with police cars. However, when travelling amongst nutters riding trikes, sports bikes and fast cars it becomes a dangerous two-way racetrack. Trucks are prohibited because many of the turns are so tight and close together, trucks could never make it around without crossing the double yellow centre lines.

The official start of the Tail of the Dragon begins in North Carolina at the intersection of NC 28 and US 129 finishing at the Tabcat Creek Bridge in Tennessee. But we were already in Tennessee, so we would be riding the Tail of the Dragon from finish to start and arrive at the Deals Gap resort after we had slayed the Dragon. The fact we were doing it in reverse didn't really matter, it was still going to be tough navigating 318 turns in 11 miles. Also, it meant that we would finish at the resort so we could chill out and relax rather than get pumped up by everyone else who was there and about to slay the Dragon.

By the time we had reached the bridge for the start, we were ready. I had distributed my luggage, making sure I didn't have too much weight on any one side or overhanging the back of the bike that would adversely affect the handling when throwing it around the corners. I had set up my GoPro camera on the handlebars to capture the whole

The Tree of Shame, Deals Gap Resort, Deals Gap, North Carolina

11 miles on HD video with a cockpit view. The bike and tires were warmed up and I was particularly focused on the task ahead. I could feel my heart rate increase and my focus become more intense as we got closer. I wanted this to be a ride to remember, I would not be doing it twice. I set off at pace and was less than a half mile behind Alex, but he got stopped by a nice policeman before he even got to the bridge. I remember seeing Alex listening to the nice policeman explaining the dangers of the road as I shot past them both at speed. Alex and I had agreed to catch up at the resort anyway, so we could exchange stories then. There was no point in my stopping. Alex had it covered and rode away with nothing more than a better understanding of the dangers of the road ahead.

I have never ridden a public road that requires such high levels of concentration for such a long period of time. To make things a little more challenging, a party of 26 trikes had already started slaying the dragon ahead of me and were spread out over the whole 11 miles. They obviously could not go as fast as motorcycles, which made the ride even more challenging as overtaking manoeuvres are extremely dangerous. On reflection, they probably did me a few favours by making me slow down at various stages on a road I had never ridden before. The high trees and dense forestry which lined both sides of the road restricted the amount of sunlight breaking through, but at speed they simply generated a sort of stroboscopic effect, which gave me a bit of a headache by the end.

Game over for Alex, Asheville, North Carolina

I was so grateful that I had slayed the Dragon without incident. The Gutzi performed admirably and got us both safely to the end (or the start in our case). I was a little shocked when I arrived at Deals Gap to see and read about those who never made it. It would have put me off riding had we started at the resort first. The *'Tree of Shame'* was particularly shocking. This tree is home to various bits of motorcycles that were once attached to someone's pride and joy. The tree tells a story all its own, and the parts hanging from its branches are from all different genres of motorcycles. No wonder the police were out in force. It was a fantastic experience to ride and, thank goodness, to survive it. Having done it once, I have absolutely no desire to repeat the performance.

For some time, Alex had been having trouble with his back. It started on the Westbound adventure, but he was able to manage his pain up until now. The Dragon had taken its toll on him. It had gotten so bad Alex could hardly ride his bike. On reaching Asheville in North Carolina his pain was so bad we took the decision to stop riding altogether and set about a plan to get us back home to Arlington. Alex had to lie down flat on the pavement to get any type of relief from his pain and he could hardly move once he had got there. We discussed various options both as individuals and as a team, but we had started this adventure together, and we were going to finish it the same way.

Alex really needed to get home as soon as possible and seek medical attention. Another night away would not be helpful. We decided that a one-way self-drive hire would be our best bet. We could load the bikes in the back and simply head for home. So that's exactly what we did. We hired a van, bought some strops from the Home Depot hardware store to secure the bikes, and headed for home.

Loading Strops for Bikes, Alex, Asheville, North Carolina

Alex really couldn't do that much, so when it came to be putting the bikes in the van, I had to ride them in without assistance. This was not a time for diligently manhandling and pushing the bikes slowly into the back of the van. No, I had to just go for it! Ride the bikes straight up the steep ramp at a speed that allowed me to retain my balance and then slam on the brakes as soon as the rear wheel had entered the loading area of the van to stop me going through the front of the cab. It was a tricky and nerve racking few minutes. I had to remove the seat from Alex's BMW as I couldn't reach the floor. Because of a serious motorcycle accident I suffered as a teenager, where I broke my back and severed my sciatic nerve on the left-hand side, my balance overall has not been the greatest even with both feet flat on the ground. So, this event was a bit of a challenge for me. I managed to get both bikes in without dropping either of them or smashing into the front of the cab. I didn't even want to think about what we would have done had something gone wrong.

Loading the Bikes in the Hire Van, Alex, Asheville, North Carolina

We set off as soon as the bikes were secured and drove 485 miles straight back home to Virginia. We arrived in Arlington at 04:15am (Tuesday). By the time we off-loaded the bikes, which was another interesting and nerve-racking moment for me, and then dropped off the truck in the Penske yard, we had been up exactly 24 hours. Alex then drove the truck, and I followed him in my car to the Penske

Back at the Apartment, Penske Hire Van, Arlington, Virginia

depot. Alex was oblivious to the formidable chain guarding the entrance of the parking lot, designed to prevent truck theft. Unfortunately, the chain was not much of a deterrent. It never stopped Alex from parking our truck in the lot, because he didn't see the chain until he hit it and took it out. All we could do was laugh. We were punch drunk at that stage. In his defence, it was dark, he was injured and tired. Fortunately, there was no chain reaction!

This was not the end we wanted, but it was absolutely the right one under the circumstances. It was great that we finished the adventure together, exactly in the same place we had started from, 27 days ago. We had made it back safely with the bikes. We had completed 227 miles and spent five hours and 50 minutes in the saddle. Then we spent another seven hours in the truck covering another 485 miles.

Both Alex and I were sad to be back home, even though Alex was in excruciating pain. I even shed a few tears once we had got back to my apartment. Reflecting on the past 27 days was simply awesome, and we both agreed we would do it all again in a heartbeat. Even the seven-hour van drive on the last day. That said, we had already discussed our next trip which would take us south and give us the opportunity to revisit Nashville, because we just had to go there again.

Pose for a Final Photograph, Nigel & Alex, Arlington, Virginia

The Route 66 Adventure had been an amazing experience on so many fronts for both of us. The riding, the friendships, the scenery and of course the people we met along the way and the shared experiences we had. No money could substitute such an awesome experience. Riding a motorcycle for 27 consecutive days was the same as having

27 different adventures back-to-back. It was inspiring and spurred us on towards a bigger and much longer adventure that would occur in 2016.

Overall, Alex and I had completed 7,024 miles on two wheels with a total of 7,509 miles altogether (12,085Kms). We had visited 18 states, four of them twice. Paul and Ian had made it to Pontiac and were planning on arriving in Chicago the same day we got back to Arlington (Tuesday September 24th). The Eastbound venture and the overall Route 66 Adventure was officially concluded. This one huge adventure that included seven individual ventures and three separate team efforts.

Chapter 7
Post Adventure Wrap Up - Fun Facts & Blog

Having parked the Gutzi back in the apartment garage, I eventually hit the sack at 5am (Tuesday 24th). Later that morning, it felt very strange to be waking up in my own bed. There would be no riding today. The Route 66 Adventure was over. All the planning and logistics had worked perfectly, and I could tick off the #1 item on my bucket list. I felt quite sad once again, knowing that it was over, but the sense of achievement lifted my spirit, and I knew that the memories we made would endure for years to come. That was a very satisfying feeling for sure. We had fallen into a routine, making riding a lifestyle, and now the reality of the trip being over was sinking in.

I had calculated that Alex and I had spent some 135 hours and 58 minutes riding our bikes. This was assumed to be pretty accurate, as the time was taken daily from the Moto Guzzi on-board computer. It was one of the few things on the Gutzi that never broke down. Though, you never can tell with Italian electrics. That made our average speed just over 55 mph for the whole adventure, the most common speed limit in the USA. Paul and Ian concluded their adventure with a trip to Milwaukee and the Harley Davidson Museum on Wednesday 25th September. Much the same way as Alex and I started our adventure in York, Pennsylvania, at the Harley Davidson factory. It was amusing to hear from Paul that they too had difficulty trying to find the start point of Route 66 on Adams Street, downtown Chicago.

My blog site had received some 5,385 views, so I was pleased about that too. When I finally closed the Blog down a year later, we had received 7,660 views. We had a couple of ups and downs and breakdowns, but these are all key ingredients of a great motorcycle adventure. Would I do it again? Yes, absolutely. However, I would select a slightly different route next time as there is so much more to see in the USA. I would also consider doing it on a different bike. Maybe even a Harley. There is no doubt that the roads and highways in the USA are made for Harleys. The Gutzi is a small-town bike at heart. Long distances are not its forte. However, it got me there and back in style. It was an awesome ride that drew a lot of attention wherever we went, just as I knew it would. We would remain a team for the next five years and some 30,000+ miles before the Gutzi retired to a new home in Ohio. I never want to sell any of my bikes, but storage space is a premium, and I needed the space to accommodate my brand-new 2018 Triumph Bonneville T120.

Alex saw his doctor the day after we got home and 10 days later, he was under the knife having a discectomy on his back. An old school rugby injury had come back to haunt him. The operation was a complete success, and he was released from hospital the day after surgery, completely free of pain and without the need to follow up with physical therapy.

On Thursday, September 26th, Ian left his Harley in Chicago and returned to New Zealand. Meanwhile, Paul got ready to ride back to Washington for me to resell the Kawasaki. Unfortunately, a very close friend of Paul's had passed away in New Zealand and Paul had to depart urgently to preside over the funeral. Luckily, he somehow sold the Kawasaki before he left Chicago on Friday 27th. Once again, not the ending that was planned for Paul, but the right one under the circumstances. Paul's departure to New Zealand effectively sealed off the Kiwi Route 66 Adventure. I painstakingly spent over 100 hours reviewing hundreds of photos and 80 Go-Pro videos to create eight short videos, each lasting between 20 to 30 minutes as an immediate memory of the adventure.

In the first quarter of 2022, I realised that 2023 would be the 10th anniversary of this Route 66 Adventure. I would have loved to have relived the experience and done the trip again. However, from other life events, I was acutely aware that things are never the same second time around and the logistics and effort involved in trying to replicate such an adventure, or anything like it, would have been enormous. I drafted a proposal for an anniversary motorcycle adventure for several friends who couldn't make the 2013 trip, but life got in the way, and I never followed through with it, as it was really difficult for anyone to commit. Therefore, I settled for writing this book as a permanent memento of the adventure. I reviewed the eight videos, the archived Go Pro videos, plus the hundreds of photographs we had taken before I put pen to paper.

It made me smile that Alex and I were the only nutters that did Route 66 twice and back-to-back. Although a true American adventure, Alex was the only American on the trip and because he had been exposed to Kiwi English for the eight months preceding the trip, he was duly nominated as the teams' language interpreter, navigator, and hotel booking clerk. He was the only person riding a European 1200cc Bavarian Tractor. Which to most Kiwis was very un-American, thinking all Americans rode Harleys.

In Chapter 4, as the Westbound Crew, we thought it would take us three weeks and we would travel some 5500 miles. However, before S3 had even arrived in the USA, Alex and I had guesstimated that any round-trip Route 66 Adventure with a few deviations, would take about three weeks (21 days), and we would clock up around 7,500 miles averaging 357 miles a day. The actual dates turned out to be 29th August through 23rd September (26 days) and we had travelled 7,509 miles, which included the 485 miles we did in a truck. So, we were surprisingly close to the distance, but way off on the days. However, considering we had two days in Santa Fe for the BMW breakdown and another two days in LA for the transfer of crews, then that brings our estimate to within a day. These non-travelling days brought down the average to 288 miles a day. Not only that, but these no travelling days were also important rest days. What was surprising was our average speed of 55 MPH. We had a couple of sprint sessions where our average speed was over 70 MPH, but these were exceptional and definitely not the norm. We spent most of our time riding on normal roads and through towns. Clearly riding a lot faster than we should have!

It had taken us 15 days to travel west, yet only just over half that (eight days) to travel back east. The route was more direct heading back home, and we were knocking out high mileage days compared to our trek west. So, it was different.

Notwithstanding Alex's back issue, we found it much easier on our bodies going west as we transited through the four different times zones. Gaining an hour is much nicer than losing one. Also, coming back east, it caught us out in Albuquerque, which resulted in a later than usual start. When you lose an hour, you mentally seem to be behind from the get-go.

Over the whole adventure, Alex and I had spent over five and a half days sat in the saddles of our motorcycles. That is a long time to spend in one position. But when you consider that we would have been travelling at an average speed of 55 MPH, that is a massive amount of concentration time, too.

The map with the squiggly black lines and circles at the end of this chapter represents the route and stop overs Alex and I took - as I understood it when I mapped it out in 2013. Yet, only after writing this book and closely examining the photos and videos did I discover the subtle deviation in the roads we traveled, contrasting with the route I had previously thought we had followed. An example is when Alex and I rode from Arkansas into Tennessee, and we intersected Illinois when we crossed over the Ohio river. It looks on the map that we deviated slightly south going into Kentucky, but we didn't. Not a huge deal, but it speaks to memory fade and the experiences each of us would have had. We all did and saw the same things, but what we remember can be different. What is clear on this map is the parts of the adventure Alex and I did twice. The stretch of road between Santa Rosa, New Mexico, and Tulsa, Oklahoma. A distance of 550 miles, just over 7% of the total distance we had travelled.

We had visited 18 states, four of them twice. Even if the ones we had visited twice were different states, we still would have fallen short of half of the lower 48 states. This clearly illustrates how massive the United States of America really is. Our total distance travelled is greater than Tunis, Tunisia to Cape Town, South Africa (6,765 miles) or a return trip from Lisbon, Portugal to Moscow, Russia (5,708 miles). In New Zealand terms, it is the equivalent of travelling from Cape Reinga to Bluff and back again three times (7,698 miles).

The 7,509-mile route taken by Nige and Alex with the 26 night stops. Sid, Surtz, and Shag (Westbound Team) and Paul and Ian (Eastbound Team) had a slight variation either side of this route. 1. Thurs 29 Aug Clarksburg WV 2. Fri 30 - Indianapolis IL 3. Sat 31 - Pontiac IL 4. Sun 1 - Rolla MO 5. Mon 2 - Tulsa OK 6. Tues 3 - Amarillo TX 7. Wed 4 - Santa Fe NM 8. Thurs 5 - Santa Fe NM 9. Fri 6 - Durango CO 10. Sat 7 - Orem UT 11. Sun 8 - Ely NV 12. Mon 9 - Lake Tahoe CA 13. Tues 10 - Monterey CA 14. Wed 11 - Ojai CA 15. Thurs 12 - Los Angeles CA 16. Fri 13 - Los Angeles LA 17. Sat 14 - Los Angeles CA 18. Sun 15 - Needles CA 19. Mon 16 - Flagstaff AZ 20 Tues 17 - Albuquerque NM 21. Wed 18 - Amarillo TX 22. Thurs 19 - Tulsa OK 23. Fri 20 - Mountain Home AR 24. Sat 21 - Nashville TN 25. Sun 22 - Crossville TN 26. Mon 23 - Travelled all day and night 27. Tues 23 - Arrived home 4:15am

Route 66 – A Guiding Light

The Route and Night Stops (as roughly remembered by Nigel)

Blog Site Commentary (unedited)

Comments:

ALISON GOODWIN| Reply28.08.2013 09.40

Have an exciting Adventure ..enjoy xx

DAWN GRAHAM| Reply28.08.2013 09.42

Brilliant! We'll drink to your trip when the Ulster Bunny gets back Good luck to you all. How did you manage all that planning without a woman on the team? Dx

ELAINE LEWIS| Reply28.08.2013 12.02

Hi Nigel and friends,hope you all have a wonderfull journey,and a safe one,good luck to you all. xxxxxx

NEIL WINDROSS| Reply28.08.2013 15.15

To 'The Kiwi Route 66 Adventure Team' I will follow your adventures with interest,... have a successful trip! Looks like very thirsty work, that planning 😊

PAM AB (OF PAUL AB - EASTWARD WILD HOG)| Reply28.08.2013 16.16

Go 'Westward The Wild Hogs' . May your bucket lists be fulfilled on this one.

PAULINE (LEEDS)| Reply28.08.2013 17.14

What an amazing trip. Have a fabulous time.

COREY WYNNE| Reply28.08.2013 21.01

Just got the link; I am very jealous! . Nige….you couldn't have picked up a reliable Beamer?? Don't know about your choice of bike mate. Ride Safe.

BLUE| Reply28.08.2013 21.27

Don't take any badmouthing of the "Beemer with a hard on". Braless Guzzis have no soul, relying on Teutonic perfection and reliability. Feel the noise Nige!

SID| Reply28.08.2013 21.34

Like this page - have to - living the dream

SID| Reply28.08.2013 21.42

Route 66 – A Guiding Light

In Nashville now - about to go down town a sample some music and a cool libation.Good riding up to here - done Barber museum, JD distillery, and about 8 bars LG

NIGE| Reply28.08.2013 23.05

Thanks everyone for your comments. Will keep you in the loop!

BOB MORGAN| Reply29.08.2013 04.11

This trip is easy, try the Brynglas tunnel at 5pm on a Friday.

That's mission impossible.

Have a trip boyos.

SUE HOPKINS| Reply29.08.2013 22.33

Hi Nige,Have a wonderful trip! Enjoy! Sue.

EDWARD| Reply30.08.2013 07.35

Have a successful trip guys!

HEADLOCK (DAVE GREEN)| Reply30.08.2013 11.48

living through you on this one!

CAROL| Reply30.08.2013 16.08

Hi Nige, wishing you all a fab trip!!! Enjoy every minute & keep safe… All our love & the very best of wishes xxx

GAYNS & RICH| Reply30.08.2013 18.54

Nige, may the force of the Welsh be with you. It will be like riding across different continents; that's the beauty of middle America.

DON MARSHALL| Reply30.08.2013 19.10

Nigel, have a successful trip - I'm jealous

SANDY STOWELL| Reply31.08.2013 17.53

LUSH!!!!!

DAVE SAUNDERS| Reply01.09.2013 01.48

Nige, Sid, Neil, and the rest of the crew. Have a safe and fun trip and watch out for the locals!!

PAM| Reply01.09.2013 23.49

Mate! That's my home State: Illinois. The heartland of America!! Land of Lincoln! Now you know why you like me so much!! Pam (I'm 'pleased to oblige', Nige)

TALEI| Reply02.09.2013 11.03

Have a successful adventure guys!

PAUL AB| Reply02.09.2013 16.41

Route 66 – A Guiding Light

Hi Buddy, it looks and sounds successful. How's the ass? I notice you all are wearing jeans, are they those motorcycle jeans? Glad to hear that you missed the rain.

PAM AB| Reply02.09.2013 19.17

I think the green dinosaur is the old "Sinclair" Petrol Station dinosaur. It looks like his head from here. Ask a Yankee. A green dinosaur used to be their icon

SIMON R| Reply03.09.2013 02.16

Jealous!

ANDREA HORTON| Reply03.09.2013 02.51

Hi Guys, have a safe trip. Watch out for "Paul"

ANDREA HORTON| Reply03.09.2013 02.59

Nice moobs guys!

MIKE| Reply03.09.2013 23.06

Winslow is a must…worth it just for the Photo…:D….(Oklahoma City sure looked pretty…:D

NIGE| Reply04.09.2013 02.14

Hey, all good. Sinclair is correct and my ass thanks. Jeans are normal ones. Riding in the American way is liberating, if a little risky!

PAUL AB| Reply04.09.2013 02.52

It looks like you guys are having a ball. You guys have spent a lot of time in the saddle, you must all be nearly a bunch of "hard asses" by now.

IAN D| Reply05.09.2013 03.17

It looks like the weather is behaving itself. The traffic appears to be relatively light; and are the roads well maintained? Safe travels, ID.

COOPS| Reply05.09.2013 11.28

Keep the pics and comments coming. Successful to follow along.

STEVE W| Reply06.09.2013 08.55

If you have time ride up to Park City in Utah, they have a successful whiskey bar.

WENDY| Reply06.09.2013 11.15

Uncle Russ says he wishes he was riding his square four with you ! Enjoy yourselves

TALEI| Reply06.09.2013 23.33

Successful updates Nige! Sounds and looks like you guys are having an awesome time! What a successful adventure!

NIGE S | Reply07.09.2013 01.36

We are all watching and reading your comments - thank you. Sadly we cannot reply to all of them but we do really appreciate them. The Westbound Team.

BRYCE MEREDITH | Reply08.09.2013 00.40

Team am following your trip with unbridled envy. Wish I was there riding with you all as this is one of my bucket items.Enjoy the weather as its crap back here.

ALISON N PAUL | Reply08.09.2013 01.46

Hope your having the time of your lives .We are thinking of you all back home in Wales .Much Love ..Take Care xxx

BOB MORGAN | Reply08.09.2013 06.42

Looks really brill Nige. I don't think my BSA 125 Bantam would have coped with it. The only thing is, why are you riding on the wrong side of the road?

VAL | Reply08.09.2013 20.14

Happy Happy Birthday Brett.

By the sounds of it the last few weeks have been

loads of FUN and laughter.

Cheers to you all

PAUL AB | Reply08.09.2013 20.50

Hi Nige and all, looks like you are doing the hard yards which makes it enjoyable.

I am here in the States and enjoying time with my brother and sister in-law.

PAUL & STEPH RENSHAW | Reply08.09.2013 22.49

Fantastic adventure guys, ride safe and keep well. We will be following your progress eagerly. You're not missing much back here, cold and windy!!

JULIE COLLINS | Reply09.09.2013 03.30

Happy 50th Brett. Have a successful day. Julie 😀

DEAN HEIFORD | Reply09.09.2013 14.59

Say Hi to Brett and remind him it is his birthday! Steph, Dean & Aidan

BILL DEWAR09.09.2013 15.15

Hi Paul

The adventure begins!! Have a successful time my brother!! Bill

MIKE WARD | Reply10.09.2013 05.04

I'm still as jealous as all hell!

MIKE WARD | Reply10.09.2013 05.27

Successful commentary guys, Keep it coming

PAUL AB | Reply10.09.2013 16.42

It might have been a lonely road but you have successful company to do it with, priceless.

LIZA AND BROOKSIE | Reply10.09.2013 17.30

Thinking of you on such a wonderful trip and dreaming of doing it again. So many happy memories. Have fun and ride safe. 😄

PAM AB | Reply12.09.2013 16.57

The two Kiwi Eastwards are fresh and ready to ride. Paul is collecting Ian and then his Harley today. Enjoy your last few days together, Westward fellas. Pam

PAM AB | Reply15.09.2013 05.43

Go Easties!!

BRYCE MEREDITH | Reply15.09.2013 17.06

Have a safe and enjoyable ride team -

BRYCE MEREDITH | Reply15.09.2013 17.22

Ride safe team. Watching with real interest and determined to do the trip myself - with a few mates as soon as we can. Paul take lots of planning notes.

KAREN AND ROBIN TURNER | Reply15.09.2013 17.38

Be safe "brother" Paul! Hope to see you in Illinois!

MUM JOYCE & RICK | Reply15.09.2013 17.39

Will be waiting to see you in Illinois. Be Safe. God Love You!

ELAINE LEWIS | Reply16.09.2013 12.05

Hope you are all having a successful time. xx

SHAG | Reply16.09.2013 13.57

Hey guys, looks like you are making successful progress, once the luggage carrying was sorted - sounds familiar!

Keep the rubber side down, Shag

PETER | Reply16.09.2013 21.29

Hey Paul how was Grand Canyon ? Things goin well back here 😎 Peter A

SID | Reply17.09.2013 12.41

PAM AB | Reply17.09.2013 16.59

Any new tatoos yet?

Ist shift safely back home now. Looks like you fellas are getting into the swing of it now - have a successful time and thx for the company.

JOHN B | Reply 18.09.2013 02.12

Well it looks like you are having a successful time, keep enjoying big fella look foward to seee what happens next, we have donkeys in nz paul so dont worry

BROOKSIE | Reply 19.09.2013 05.41

Hey Paul could be "V for Victory" for the NZ team in SF tomorrow! Go Kiwis!

DICK GERDES | Reply 19.09.2013 10.10

Hey, guys. Hope all is well. I thoroughly enjoyed having dinner with you in Albuquerque on your return trip. Be safe.

MIKE WARD | Reply 20.09.2013 07.53

Keep on rocking and keep the shiny side up! Mike

BROOKSIE | Reply 20.09.2013 17.18

Luck is what happens when preparation meets opportunity.
(Latest from the board outside the Base Chapel)

GAYNS | Reply 21.09.2013 06.19

Nige, good to see you are still making friends wherever you go, even if they are a plastic green alligator. That steak is massive!

ALISON GOODWIN | Reply 22.09.2013 12.44

Love the shaving look Nigel,,it actually suits you !

ROWENA COLLETT | Reply 24.09.2013 22.02

Congratulations Deb and Brett!! So happy for ya's 😄

LIZA AND BROOKSIE | Reply 25.09.2013 03.54

Hi AB called in on Pam and the ginger cat last Sunday she is doing well and was cooking chicken vindaloo. Hope you are safe and enjoying your trip. Cheers!

PAM | Reply 25.09.2013 17.41

You've said all along that your Rt 66 is journey is your journey, but I don't like that Alex was nearly 'slain by the dragon'! Take Care Alex. Pam

SHAG | Reply 26.09.2013 02.27

Hey Alex, if your bike needs a service you could always ship your bike to Santa Fe and leave it with f@#king Diego!!

DAVID KORFF 26.09.2013 13.48

Hi "LITTLE GUY" . Pam told me that you have now reached Chicago!!! Awesome stuff. May you have a successful rest of your journey. God bless.
Dave (aka "BIG GUY")

About the Author
Nigel M Sainsbury

Nigel M Sainsbury Promoting First Book, Fairfax, VA, 2019

Born a Welshman, Nigel grew up in the coal mining valleys of South Wales, in the United Kingdom. An avid motorcyclist, musician and aviation professional, Nigel joined the Royal Air Force (RAF) at age 16 and served for twenty-seven years as an Aero Systems Engineer. In 2004, Nigel retired for the first time and emigrated with his family to the other side of the world to join the Royal New Zealand Air Force (RNZAF). Nigel officially became a Kiwi in 2007 and completed twelve years active service in the RNZAF. In 2016 Nigel retired a second time on completion of his tour of duty as the Defense Advisor to Canada and Air Attaché to the United States of America, located in the New Zealand Embassy in Washington, DC. Rather than return to New Zealand, Nigel married his American Fiancée, Carol, and started his own consultancy business and now lives in Fairfax, Virginia. A citizen of both the United Kingdom and New Zealand, Nigel is also a Permanent Resident of the USA. This is Nigel's fourth non-fiction book in five years.